CIVIL GOVERNMENT

What the Bible Says About Its Origin, History, Nature, and Role

Andy Sochor

with contributions by
Tim Haile

Gospel Armory
PUBLISHING

Civil Government: What the Bible Says About Its Origin, History, Nature, and Role
Copyright © 2012 by Andy Sochor

Published by:
Gospel Armory Publishing
Bowling Green, Kentucky
www.GospelArmory.com

Printed in the United States of America

ISBN: 978-0-9831046-4-3

SPECIAL THANKS

A lot of work went into this book and not all of it was done by me. Four chapters were written by Tim Haile. He was kind enough to let me use his material (these chapters are noted in the table of contents), in addition to providing feedback along the way. My mom, Eva Sochor, also spent a good deal of time doing the proofreading and editing. And of course, my wife Rachel, as a suitable help meet, kept up with the needs of the household, allowing me to focus on this project. Thank you.

TABLE OF CONTENTS

INTRODUCTION

Religion and politics are two topics that we are told should never be mixed with one another. There are brethren who cringe at any discussion of government in a sermon or Bible class that goes beyond, *"Every person is to be in subjection to the governing authorities"* (Romans 13:1), and, *"Render to Caesar the things that are Caesar's"* (Matthew 22:21). Yet there is much that the Bible has to say about *government* in addition to these oft cited passages. In fact, there is so much Bible teaching on this topic that this material will not cover everything. It is an introduction of sorts that will hopefully spur you on to reflection and further study.

In this study, we will discuss what the Bible teaches on the following matters:

- God-given natural rights
- Civil government's inherent animosity toward those rights
- The godless and rebellious origins of civil government
- The foundation for a godly society (that can function with or without government)
- The limited role for which God ordained civil government
- How civil government often acts as a minister of Satan
- Warnings against a strong, centralized government
- The inherent limitations of civil government
- Our responsibilities to our leaders and the *limits* of those responsibilities (including the responsibility to pay taxes)

- Why Christians should take advantage of our privilege to vote

Some will be turned off by a study that uses the Bible to argue political positions. But let me be clear: this book is not about *politics*, though it does address matters that are debated by politicians. It is about the the origins and role of civil government and how it affects our lives as Christians.

It is my hope that Christians will study these things and consider them carefully.

1

GOD-GIVEN RIGHTS

The Declaration of Independence speaks of certain "unalienable rights." These rights were the basis for the colonists' complaint against England, the justification for their Declaration of Independence, and later, the reason why the Constitution would so constrain the power of the federal government.

The founders of this country carefully crafted these documents. What they produced continues to be a standard for our leaders to follow and for governments around the world to emulate. While the framers of these documents are worthy of regard for their efforts and wisdom, their ideas about man's natural rights were not original with them. They borrowed ideas from others, combined them with their own wisdom and experience, and produced the documents that laid the foundation of this country.

Ultimately, everything that is good and true, when traced back to its original source, is from God. The founders recognized this about our natural rights. The Declaration of Independence states: "We hold these truths to be self-evident, that all men are created equal, that they are endowed by their Creator with certain unalienable Rights, that among these are Life, Liberty, and the pursuit of Happiness." These men believed that our natural rights — which included life, liberty, and the pursuit of happiness — were granted to us by God. As we will see in this study, the Scriptures confirm this.

The rights of life, liberty, and the pursuit of happiness can be summed up in one word — freedom. In the beginning, God made man and made him free by virtue of the fact that he was made in

God's image (Genesis 1:27). As long as man is made in God's image (which will be true until the end of time), he has the inherent right to freedom. Unfortunately, history has repeatedly shown that this freedom is often denied or restricted by those who are stronger, more powerful, more numerous, or, as is often the case, in positions of civil authority.

Before addressing some of these denials and restrictions of freedom, let us first notice from the Scriptures the ways in which God has made us free.

Freedoms Which God Has Given Man

In order to establish the fact that God made man inherently free, we will consider some passages from the beginning — the book of Genesis. Before men started to take away or restrict the freedoms of their fellow man (often through the force of civil government), all men naturally possessed certain freedoms from God.

Freedom of choice — The most basic and fundamental freedom is the freedom for one to choose what he will or will not do. God made us free moral agents. Before and after the Fall, man has had this freedom of choice.

While in the Garden, Adam received the Lord's command: "*From any tree of the garden you may eat freely; but from the tree of the knowledge of good and evil you shall not eat, for in the day that you eat from it you will surely die*" (Genesis 2:16-17). If God did not want Adam to eat of the fruit of this tree, why did He place it in the Garden at all? Why did Adam even have the option to eat of this tree when God could have easily taken the option away? It is because God wants man to *choose* to follow Him. After this sin was committed, God had to drive Adam and Eve from the

Garden so that they would not *choose* to eat of the tree of life and live forever (Genesis 3:22-24).

Later, after man's population increased, wickedness increased, so much so that God decided to destroy mankind. How did man become so wicked? He *chose* to be wicked. *"Then the Lord saw that the wickedness of man was great on the earth, and that every intent of the thoughts of his heart was only evil continually"* (Genesis 6:5). Man was wicked because his thoughts were evil. He was able to do whatever he wanted to do. But it is important to note that man's wickedness was not something inherent in him by virtue of the fact that he descended from Adam. The wickedness was a choice. The record of Noah makes this clear: *"Noah was a righteous man, blameless in his time; Noah walked with God"* (Genesis 6:9). If man is inherently sinful, how could Noah have been blameless? The answer lies in this fundamental truth: God has given us the freedom to *choose* what we will do and how we will live.

Freedom of movement — Another freedom that man has naturally from God is the freedom to move about and go wherever he chooses to go. Again, this freedom was granted in the beginning. God told Adam and Eve, *"Be fruitful and multiply, and fill the earth"* (Genesis 1:28). After the flood, Noah and his sons were told the same thing (Genesis 9:1). There were no travel restrictions placed upon man. They were all free to move about as they pleased, as God had granted this right to them.

Abram and Lot provide examples of ones who carried out this freedom: *"Now there was a famine in the land; so Abram went down to Egypt to sojourn there, for the famine was severe in the land"* (Genesis 12:10). Abram was not confined to one region. When the land in which he lived was experiencing a famine, he was perfectly free to move to Egypt.

Lot traveled with Abram for some time; but eventually, after they had left Egypt, he had to separate from Abram because they had become so prosperous that the land could not support all of their flocks and herds. When they separated from one another, Abram gave Lot the choice of which direction he desired to take. *"Lot lifted up his eyes and saw all the valley of the Jordan, that it was well watered everywhere... like the garden of the Lord... So Lot chose for himself all the valley of the Jordan, and Lot journeyed eastward. Thus they separated from each other"* (Genesis 13:10-11). Later, Lot would be taken captive by an evil king and forced to leave his home (Genesis 14:12). But as he was given this choice by Abram, Lot could choose the direction he wished to go without any government interference because of the natural right to move about that God had granted to all men from the beginning.

Freedom of speech — The freedom of speech is one of the rights we cherish in this country. God created us with the ability to communicate and share our thoughts and ideas with others. In the beginning, man was able to do this without interference or restriction from any government entity.

Communication is part of the foundation of society. If people cannot communicate, they cannot interact with one another. A free flow of ideas helps man to achieve great things. While this can often be used for good, it can also be used to achieve things of which God does not approve. This was the case when the people set out to build the Tower of Babel.

> *"Now the whole earth used the same language and the same words. It came about as they journeyed east, that they found a plain in the land of Shinar and settled there. They said to one another, 'Come, let us make bricks and burn them thoroughly.' And they used brick for stone, and they used tar for mortar. They said, 'Come, let us build for ourselves a city, and a tower whose top will reach into heaven, and let us make for*

ourselves a name, otherwise we will be scattered abroad over the face of the whole earth" (Genesis 11:1-4).

The text explicitly tells us that the people were of one language. This is significant. Not only were there no state-imposed restrictions to speech, but there were no language barriers either. Because of this, they were able to start work on this great building project.

While there may not have been anything wrong with building a tower in itself, the goal they wished to achieve was not only contrary to the will of God but was also unachievable. They would never be able to reach heaven. Furthermore, their goal of uniting mankind under one world power was in direct opposition to God's will for man from the beginning where He — not a ruling body which originated with Nimrod (Genesis 10:8-10) — would have the authority over the families of the earth.

God came down from heaven, observed what man was doing, and determined to put an end to it. But the way God put an end to it is interesting. Several things made their construction of the tower possible: resources for their materials, manual labor, plans and design for the structure, and the ability to communicate to express the plans and give orders to the workers. The one that God chose to disrupt was the last one: the ability to communicate.

Notice what God does and what He does not do. He does not take away their right to speak, even though they were using their speech in a way that was contrary to His will. They could still speak, but He confused their languages so that they would not understand one another.

There is certainly speech which is condemned by God: lying, cursing, false teaching, blasphemy, etc. But God allows man, while he is here on the earth, to speak his mind. This goes back to the freedom of choice which God gave man in the beginning. Man can choose his words and suffer the consequences of them. When man's words resulted in communication that produced the Tower of Babel, God stopped it — not by restricting the speech but by segregating the people by language. Even then, man was able to speak freely with his own people.

God gave man the right to speak and express his thoughts to others. Even in this example of rebellion, God did not revoke man's right; He simply changed their languages. By doing this, He restricted the *understanding* of others' speech (something only God can do) but left the *right to speak* in place.

Freedom of association — The right to form relationships with whomever we choose is another one of the freedoms God has given man from the beginning. This does not necessarily mean that all associations are approved by God, but the fact that God allows man to make this choice cannot be denied.

Before the flood the record says, "*The sons of God saw that the daughters of men were beautiful; and they took wives for themselves, whomever they chose*" (Genesis 6:2). Marriage is the most fundamental relationship for the human race. The people before the flood were able to enter into this relationship with *whomever they chose*. No approval from others, including a governing body, needed to be sought.

We have already noticed the example of those who set out to build the Tower of Babel in connection with the right to free speech. But the right to free association with others is seen in this example as well. "*It came about as they journeyed east, that they found a plain in the land of Shinar and settled there. They said to one another, 'Come, let us make bricks and burn them thoroughly.' [...] They said, 'Come, let us build for ourselves a city...'*" (Genesis 11:2-4). Their sin was in trying to make a name for themselves and in trying to reach heaven through their own means. There was no sin committed in settling in one place and working together. Man, without government interference, is free to associate with whomever he chooses.

The opposite is also true. Man can choose to sever or deny association with whomever he chooses. When Abram and Lot journeyed together and their flocks and herds were so numerous that the land could not sustain them, they chose to separate from one another (Genesis 13:5-9). There was no government order that demanded they separate. There was no environmental protection regulation that was violated by their staying together. They chose this for their mutual benefit (and that of their feuding herdsmen).

From the beginning, God has granted man the freedom to enter into various associations that pertain to every part of our lives: marriage, work, residence, etc.

Freedom to use natural resources — In the beginning, *"God blessed them; and God said to them, 'Be fruitful and multiply, and fill the earth, and subdue it; and rule over the fish of the sea and over the birds of the sky and over every living thing that moves on the earth.' Then God said, 'Behold, I have given you every plant yielding seed that is on the surface of all the earth, and every tree which has fruit yielding seed; it shall be food for you; and to every beast of the earth and to every bird of the sky and to every thing that moves on the earth which has life, I have given every green plant for food'; and it was so"* (Genesis 1:28-30).

The first man and woman were given the authority by God to use the things which He had created as they wished. They were to *"fill the earth, and subdue it."* If someone like Abel wanted to be *"a keeper of flocks,"* he could be. If someone like Cain wanted to be *"a tiller of the ground"* (Genesis 4:2), he was free to do that, as well. After the flood this freedom was restated with an additional permission given: *"Every moving thing that is alive shall be food for you; I give all to you, as I gave the green plant"* (Genesis 9:3).

The freedom for man to use the natural resources present in God's creation can be clearly seen in the fact that God allows man to *misuse* the things He has given. When God made everything, "*it was very good*" (Genesis 1:31) — *if* those things were used for their correct purposes. But God allows man to *choose* how he will use these blessings either for good or bad.

We see an example of this with Noah after the flood. "*Then Noah began farming and planted a vineyard. He drank of the wine and became drunk, and uncovered himself inside his tent*" (Genesis 9:20-21). The abuse of alcohol is condemned throughout Scripture. Even though it was possible for Noah to produce wine using those things which God had given, he *misused* those blessings from God. The same is true with marijuana and other drugs. Though they may be found naturally or can be produced using natural ingredients, not every use of these things is approved by God. Yet God gave man the choice and the freedom to use the creation as he saw fit.

Freedom to own property — Another one of the rights that naturally exists for man is the right to own property. Early on we read of Abram who was able to acquire property and relocate to another place without giving up his possessions. "*Abram took Sarai his wife and Lot his nephew, and all their possessions which they had accumulated, and the persons which they had acquired in Haran, and they set out for the land of Canaan; thus they came to the land of Canaan*" (Genesis 12:5).

In fact, not only did Abram have the right to own property, he had the right to become very wealthy. "*Now Abram was very rich in livestock, in silver and in gold*" (Genesis 13:2). "*Now Lot, who went with Abram, also had flocks and herds and tents. And the land could not sustain them while dwelling together, for their possessions were so great that they were not able to remain together*" (Genesis 13:5-6). There is nothing *inherently* wrong with one becoming wealthy. From the beginning, without interference or permission from any government body, men like Abram, Job, and others were able to own great amounts of property.

This right to own property even exists when a civil leader challenges one's ownership of a particular piece of property. *"But Abraham complained to Abimelech because of the well of water which the servants of Abimelech had seized"* (Genesis 21:25). Abimelech was king of Gerar (Genesis 20:2). Yet his position as a king did not give him or his servants the right to seize the well that rightfully belonged to Abraham, the one who dug the well (Genesis 21:30). A man has the right to keep that for which he labors.

When Sarah died, Abraham needed a place to bury his wife. So he purchased the cave of Machpelah from Ephron the Hittite for four hundred shekels of silver (Genesis 23:3-20). Ephron owned the land and had the right to sell it (Genesis 23:9). When they agreed upon a price, Abraham paid it; and the land was *"deeded over"* to him (Genesis 23:17,20). This was done *"in the presence of the sons of Heth, before all who went in at the gate of the city"* (Genesis 23:18), showing that this agreement, transaction, and ownership of the property was something that all the people recognized.

Freedom to defend one's own — The right to self-defense and to protect one's family and property is another fundamental right that man has had since the beginning. To murder or otherwise maliciously bring violence upon one's fellow man is inherently evil (Genesis 9:6). But protecting oneself or one's own from such harm is a natural right.

When Lot and his possessions were captured by the kings who waged war against Sodom (Genesis 14:8-12), Abram immediately set out to deliver him.

"When Abram heard that his relative had been taken captive, he led out his trained men, born in his house, three hundred and eighteen, and went in pursuit as far as Dan. He divided his forces against them by night, he and his servants, and defeated them, and pursued them as far as Hobah, which is north of Damascus. He brought back all the goods, and also brought back his relative Lot with his possessions, and also the women, and the people" (Genesis 14:14-16).

Abram did not live under a human king. During this time of the patriarchs, he, as the head of his household, was in authority over his household and under the authority of God alone. As a free man of God, he had the right to rescue Lot. In fact, he was already prepared to do this, as he had three hundred and eighteen men who were already trained for battle. Why would this great man of faith have such an army ready to do battle if he did not have the right to defend himself and his own?

Some Christians will argue that God's people today should not exercise this right of self-defense. Even if their argument was true, that does not mean that the natural right of self-defense, or self-preservation, no longer exists. Those who argue against self-defense must say that one should exercise *restraint* rather than defend themselves or others from harm. Why would restraint be necessary? It is because self-preservation is natural and normal, even for God's people under the new covenant. This is why the Christians in Jerusalem fled in the face of persecution (Acts 8:1) and why Paul *"fought with wild beasts at Ephesus"* (1 Corinthians 15:32), rather than passively suffer harm. The desire for self-preservation is inherent in man and the right to defend one's own has existed from the beginning of God's creation.

Freedom to worship — The most important right which God has given man is the freedom to worship Him. In the beginning, man had direct access to God, as Adam and Eve would have company with Him in the Garden (Genesis 3:8). After they sinned and were driven out, they no longer had this regular, direct, personal contact (Genesis 3:23-24).

However, even though the preferred conditions of the Garden were lost, man was still able to approach God in worship. Immediately after the Fall, Genesis records Adam and Eve's two sons worshiping God.

> *"So it came about in the course of time that Cain brought an offering to the Lord of the fruit of the ground. Abel, on his part also brought of the firstlings of his flock and of their fat portions. And the Lord had regard for Abel and for his offering; but for Cain and for his offering He had no regard. So Cain became very angry and his countenance fell"* (Genesis 4:3-5).

Cain and Abel were both able to worship God in the way they saw fit. This, of course, did not mean that any form of worship they offered would be acceptable. But God had certainly given them the freedom to choose how they would worship. At this time there was no government to grant them the freedom of religion. But they did not need it. Freedom of religion is a God-given right to all human beings.

Not only does man have the freedom to worship in the manner he sees fit; but other choices about worship naturally belong to man to make, hopefully, according to God's will. Notice the example of Abraham:

> *"So Abraham rose early in the morning and saddled his donkey, and took two of his young men with him and Isaac his son; and he split wood for the burnt offering, and arose and went to the place of which God had told him. On the third day Abraham raised his eyes and saw the place from a distance. Abraham said to his young*

men, 'Stay here with the donkey, and I and the lad will go over there; and we will worship and return to you'" (Genesis 22:3-5).

Abraham was free to worship God in the manner in which he determined (using *"wood for the burnt offering"*). But there were other details he was able to choose. He had the freedom to worship with those of his choosing (he and Isaac would go, but the young men would not), in the place of his choosing (which was the place where God told him), and at the time of his choosing (he departed the morning after the Lord called him). There were no restrictions that hindered Abraham from worshiping God how, when, where, and with whom he chose. He was free to decide these things, as all men have the God-given right to choose these things as well. Again, the *right* to worship does not mean unconditional *approval* from God for various religious practices; but the right exists nonetheless.

Conclusion

The Founders of this country were correct in their belief that our rights come from our Creator, not from any human government. These rights and freedoms are inherent in our being human and are therefore unalienable. Man is not dependent upon his government granting him a right to speak, move about, own property, defend his own, or worship God.

Yet so many in our society misunderstand this. They believe that government, not God, is the entity which grants them their rights. Or — what may be more common among religious people — they believe that God-given rights only apply when the government permits us to retain those rights. Christians may make an exception here for the right to worship God. But aside from that, many seem to have the idea that the only rights we have are the ones that God and government *agree* that we should have.

The reality is that the government does not grant rights (though many mistakenly believe that it does). God grants us our natural rights. What government does, all too often, is restrict or deny those God-given rights. The next chapter will discuss how the Bible describes this being done throughout history.

2

GOVERNMENT'S HISTORY OF TAKING MAN'S RIGHTS

If God made man free, then there are only three ways in which our natural rights can be restricted.

1. ***God can take away the rights He has given.*** That which the Lord gives to us, He has the power to take away from us (Job 1:21). However, as we have studied in the previous chapter, God allows us the freedom to do even those things which are displeasing to Him. Having *a right* (the freedom or power) to do a thing does not necessarily mean it is *right* to do it. God allows us to live as we choose but holds us accountable for our actions (2 Corinthians 5:10).

2. ***We can choose not to exercise our rights.*** In 1 Corinthians 8, Paul argued that a Christian has a right to eat meat that has been sacrificed to idols (1 Corinthians 8:4, 8). He even referred to this as a *"liberty"* (1 Corinthians 8:9). In this case, obviously, the natural right existed as God had given man permission to eat meat since the end of the flood (Genesis 9:3). But more than a natural right, Paul said that a Christian may eat this meat without committing a sin (1 Corinthians 8:8). However, he acknowledged that *"not all men have this knowledge"* (1 Corinthians 8:7). These

individuals would sin by eating this meat. So Paul decided to refrain from eating meat, choosing not to exercise his natural and spiritual right, so as not to cause a brother to stumble (1 Corinthians 8:13). In this case, the right itself still exists. We just make the choice to refrain from acting upon that right.

3. ***Our rights can be taken or restricted by force, often by those in positions of civil authority.*** Since God grants us our natural rights, only He can take them away. Yet governments constantly try to force us into surrendering those rights, whether it is something small like restricting what type of structure you can build on your property, to much more severe offenses such as imprisoning, torturing, and killing dissidents. Though man's natural, God-given rights remain, governments often use force to persuade one not to exercise those rights (thus giving the appearance of those rights being taken away).

In this chapter, we will look at some Bible examples of civil authorities attempting to restrict man from exercising his natural rights. By doing this, we will see that this is not a modern problem but an ancient one — and one that is inherent in the institution of government.

The Capture of Lot — After telling us about Abram and Lot departing from one another and Lot settling in Sodom, the Bible contains the record of the king of Sodom and his allies going to war with five other kings (Genesis 14:1-3). The king of Sodom and his allies had served Chedorlaomer, king of Elam, for twelve years. But in the thirteenth year of this involuntary servitude, they rebelled against him (Genesis 14:4). The end result of this rebellion was defeat for the king of Sodom. He was killed when he fled and fell into the tar pits, and his city was plundered by the opposing army (Genesis 14:10-11).

Lot was living in Sodom at the time when all of this was transpiring. When the king of Sodom was defeated and Chedorlaomer and his allies plundered the city, *"They also took Lot, Abram's nephew, and his possessions and departed, for he was living in Sodom"* (Genesis 14:12).

Prior to this, Lot was free to move about as he chose and could own property (so much property that he and Abram had to separate from one another). But now his freedom of movement was taken away (he was taken captive and forced to go along with his captors); and his freedom to own property was taken away (his possessions were confiscated by his captors). Without interference from civil government, Lot was able to go where he pleased, stay where he wished, and obtain great wealth. But when a hostile government became involved, these God-given rights were taken from him.

The Egyptian Bondage — When we think of the Egyptian bondage, we typically think of the Israelites' bondage in Egypt. We will notice that example next. But there was another Egyptian bondage that came first. In this example, the ones enslaved were not foreigners like the Israelites; they were the Egyptians themselves.

During the years of famine in Egypt, the Egyptians went to Joseph in order to get food. The Egyptian government had plenty of provisions, thanks to Joseph interpreting Pharaoh's dreams and gathering food during the seven years of plenty (Genesis 41:25-32, 46-49). When the Egyptians came to Joseph, they were expected to *buy* the food. They first used their money to do so (Genesis 47:13-14). When that was gone they traded their livestock for food (Genesis 47:15-17). But the famine continued, and they had nothing left to trade for food. Yet they came to Joseph once again.

> *"When that year was ended, they came to* [Joseph] *the next year and said to him, 'We will not hide from my lord that our money is all spent, and the cattle are my lord's. There is nothing left for my lord except our bodies and our lands. Why should we die before your eyes, both we and our land? Buy us and our land for food, and we and our land will be slaves to Pharaoh. So give us seed, that we may live and not die, and that the land may not be desolate'"* (Genesis 47:18-19).

It should be noted that this was an extreme set of circumstances that led to the Egyptians *offering* to become slaves. Furthermore, we should remember that a *godly man* (Joseph) was in charge of the government operations here. We will notice why this is important in just a moment. First, read what happened after the Egyptians offered to become Pharaoh's slaves.

> *"So Joseph bought all the land of Egypt for Pharaoh, for every Egyptian sold his field, because the famine was severe upon them. Thus the land became Pharaoh's. As for the people, he removed them to the cities from one end of Egypt's border to the other"* (Genesis 47:20-21).

We can assume that Joseph had the best of intentions and that he wanted to perform well under Pharaoh and help the Egyptians as best he could under the circumstances. Yet this righteous man, in trying to save the Egyptian people, removed them from their lands and forced them to relocate to the cities. We can surely see the reasoning behind this. If the Egyptian government was going to have to take care of these people, it would be easier to do so if they were gathered together in cities rather than spread out over the countryside. So we certainly cannot fault Joseph, especially since the Egyptians *asked* to be enslaved to Pharaoh. But as a result of this, their rights to own property (they lost their lands) and to move about freely (they were forced to live in the cities) were taken away.

There is an important point we need to take from this example. Even a godly man with good intentions acting rationally, when he is operating as an agent of civil authority, can restrict the natural rights that man has from God. How much more when you have wicked, vengeful, and irrational rulers! Government, by its very nature, works to restrict the rights of the people. A godly ruler does not change this; he only limits the negative impact.

The Israelites' Bondage in Egypt — The Egyptian bondage with which we are most familiar is the period of time when the Israelites were in bondage in Egypt. The enslavement of the children of Israel began as a result of the new king being fearful that the people might exercise their God-given right to associate with those of their choosing in a way that would be problematic to the regime.

> "*Now a new king arose over Egypt, who did not know Joseph. He said to his people, 'Behold, the people of the sons of Israel are more and mightier than we. Come, let us deal wisely with them, or else they will multiply and in the event of war, they will also join themselves to those who hate us, and fight against us and depart from the land.' So they appointed taskmasters over them to afflict them with hard labor. And they built for Pharaoh storage cities, Pithom and Raamses*" (Exodus 1:8-11).

Of course, the Israelites would eventually leave Egypt — not in the manner that Pharaoh feared (by joining with Egypt's enemies and turning against them), but through divine deliverance that Pharaoh would fight so hard against. It was not until *after* the people were afflicted that God set the plan for their deliverance into motion (Exodus 2:23-25). As long as they were free in Egypt to live, work, multiply, and serve God, the people were content to remain; and God allowed them to take advantage of such favorable conditions to strengthen their numbers. When oppression came, the Israelites expressed the natural response of man in the face of such — sighing, groaning, and crying out. They desired freedom from such oppression. God would provide it.

There are several things that Pharaoh did in order to restrict the natural rights of the children of Israel. Civil governments have continued to do these same types of things throughout history.

- **Forced labor** — We already noticed that Pharaoh *"appointed taskmasters over them to afflict them with hard labor"* (Exodus 1:11). This would be bad enough. But more than just making them work hard, they did so in an attempt to demoralize them. *"The Egyptians compelled the sons of Israel to labor rigorously; and they made their lives bitter with hard labor in mortar and bricks and at all kinds of labor in the field, all their labors which they rigorously imposed on them"* (Exodus 1:13-14). If the Egyptians simply wanted certain tasks completed, they could have paid a fair wage; and people (both Israelites and Egyptians) would have agreed to work. But this is not what was happening. A fair wage was not being offered in order to entice men to choose this work. They were *compelled* to do the work and did not receive just compensation for it. Furthermore, when Pharaoh became angry over the request to allow the people to go into the wilderness to worship God, he decided to *increase* their labor without increasing their compensation in an effort to keep them busy enough that they would *"pay no attention"* to Moses (Exodus 5:4-9).

- **Physical abuse** — Bible believers will certainly agree that civil government ought to punish evildoers (Romans 13:4). Yet the Israelites were not afflicted for any crime they had committed (at least not any crime against a legitimate law). They were being abused in order to compel them to remain in submission to their oppressive Egyptian masters (Exodus 1:11; 2:11; 5:14). The abuse was so severe that the Israelites complained to Moses that his efforts had *"put a sword in* [the Egyptians'] *hand to kill* [them]" (Exodus 5:21).

- **Infanticide** — Given the fact that the Egyptians were willing to beat and threaten the lives of the Israelites, it is not surprising that they were willing to kill infants as well. Because Pharaoh feared the growing numbers of the Israelites, he ordered the midwives, *"When you are helping the Hebrew women to give birth and see them upon the birthstool, if it is a son, then you shall put him to death; but if it is a daughter, then she shall live"* (Exodus 1:16). Pharaoh believed that as king, he had the power to determine who was worthy of the right to life and who was not. The right to life is granted by God, not some human ruler. The midwives understood this. *"But the midwives feared God, and did not do as the king of Egypt had commanded them, but let the boys live"* (Exodus 1:17). Human history is filled with evil rulers carrying out heinous acts of infanticide, abortion, genocide, and other forms of mass murder, believing that their position gives them the authority of God in determining who has the right to life and who does not. Pharaoh's attempt here is just one example of this.

- **Restricted freedom of movement** — A free people may move about how they wish, just as we noticed in the previous chapter with the examples of Noah and his sons (Genesis 9:1), and Abram and Lot (Genesis 12:10; 13:10-11). In Egypt, Moses had to request permission from Pharaoh for the people to *"go a three days' journey into the wilderness"* (Exodus 5:3). Pharaoh, of course, would not let them go.
- **Restricted freedom to worship** — Tied to the restriction on movement was Pharaoh's restriction on worship. Moses said to Pharaoh, *"Thus says the Lord, the God of Israel, 'Let My people go that they may celebrate a feast to Me in the wilderness'"* (Exodus 5:1). The purpose of their request to go into the wilderness was to *"sacrifice to the Lord"* (Exodus 5:3). Yet Pharaoh placed restrictions upon their worship, not allowing them to travel to the place necessary for such. Once the plagues had started, Pharaoh tried to allow the Israelites to worship God, not according to divine instructions, but according to Pharaoh's regulations — they would be allowed to worship *within* the land, but not in the wilderness (Exodus 8:25-27); they could *"not go very far away"* instead of a three days' journey (Exodus 8:28); only the men would be allowed to go (Exodus 10:8-11); or that they could go but the livestock (thus, the sacrifices) would have to remain behind (Exodus 10:24). On several occasions, Pharaoh said he would allow the people to go and worship, only to change his mind (Exodus 8:8-15; 8:25-32; 9:27-35; 10:16-20). But in these examples, he was willing to allow worship, but only the worship that he determined would be acceptable.

The example of the Egyptian bondage of the Israelites shows us a human ruler who put men into forced labor, abused them, sought to kill those who were deemed to be a threat to him (even though they were innocent infants), and regulated the movement and worship of those who lived in his land. It is not hard to see how civil governments do the same sort of things today.

The Reign of Saul — The reign of Saul, the first king over Israel, contains several examples of hostility toward man's God-given rights. This should not be surprising, considering that Samuel warned the people that this would happen. After telling the people that the king would *take* their sons, daughters, lands, grain, vineyards, servants, and flocks, the prophet warned: *"And you yourselves will become his servants"* (1 Samuel 8:17).

This is the natural progression of human government. As its power grows, its claim over the lives of the citizens also grows, thus leading to oppression and slavery. When this would happen to the Israelites and they would *"cry out in that day because of* [their] *king..., and the Lord* [would] *not answer* [them] *in that day"* (1 Samuel 8:18). Why not? Their government would inevitably grow and become hostile toward freedom. Though they were warned, they chose this anyway. When people choose to live under oppression, then they will suffer the consequences for it.

Notice some of the abuses and failures of King Saul:

• **His foolish order** — In an arrogant display of selfishness, Saul *"put the people under oath, saying, 'Cursed be the man who eats food before evening, and until I have avenged myself on my enemies.' So none of the people tasted food"* (1 Samuel 14:24). After this the people entered a forest and found *"a flow of honey"* (v. 26). But no one ate of it, despite their hunger, because they feared the king. What right did Saul have to restrict the free use of the natural blessings provided by God? Some will say today that this would have been perfectly within his right as king, just as some today believe rulers have some divinely-given authority to keep people from using things like raw milk. But notice what Jonathan says after he eats of the honey (unaware of the order and having no reason to think there may be such a foolish order) and is reminded of the curse by the other men: "*My father has troubled the land. See now, how my eyes have brightened because I tasted a little of this honey. How much more, if only the people had eaten freely today of the spoil of their enemies which they found! For now the slaughter of the Philistines has not been great*" (1 Samuel 14:29-30). The blessings that are given by God ought to be enjoyed freely without interference from a misguided human statute. Jonathan understood that his father had "*troubled the land*" by not allowing the people to take advantage of what was before them.

- **His failure to fulfill his legitimate role as king** — The people wanted a king, in part, so that he could "*go out before* [them] *and fight* [their] *battles*" (1 Samuel 8:20). The Scriptures teach that *bearing the sword* is a legitimate function of civil government (Romans 13:4). Yet when the people needed him to fulfill this role the most, he was unwilling to do so. When Goliath, the giant of the Philistines, challenged Israel to send *one man* to fight him, the result of which would determine whether the Israelites would serve the Philistines or vice versa, Saul refused to fight (1 Samuel 17:8-9). "*Again the Philistine said, 'I defy the ranks of Israel this day; give me a man that we may fight together.' When Saul and all Israel heard these words of the Philistine, they were dismayed and greatly afraid*" (1 Samuel 17:10-11). We are familiar with the account of David coming and fighting with Goliath, knowing that God would be with him and would allow him to be victorious (1

Samuel 17:32-37). Saul, the king who was to fight their battles (1 Samuel 8:20) and was head and shoulders above the people (1 Samuel 9:2), should have been the one to challenge Goliath; but he was unwilling.

- **The slaughter of the priests at Nob** — One of the more egregious crimes of Saul came against the priests of Nob. He accused Ahimelech the priest of conspiring with David against the king (1 Samuel 22:11-13). Ahimelech declared his innocence, indicating that he knew nothing about these charges (1 Samuel 22:14-15). *"But the king said, 'You shall surely die, Ahimelech, you and all your father's household!' And the king said to the guards who were attending him, 'Turn around and put the priests of the Lord to death…' But the servants of the king were not willing to put forth their hands to attack the priests of the Lord. Then the king said to Doeg, 'You turn around and attack the priests.' And Doeg the Edomite turned around and attacked the priests, and he killed that day eighty-five men who wore the linen ephod. And he struck Nob the city of the priests with the edge of the sword, both men and women, children and infants…"* (1 Samuel 22:16-19). Saul had no proof that Ahimelech did anything wrong, only a suspicion. But for one in a position of power who views himself as being above the law and believes his highest priority is retaining power, mere suspicion was enough. He charged the innocent priest, tried him in his own mind, then executed his own perverted form of justice against him. Even when his servants were unwilling to carry out this order, they did not oppose the king. Saul then found someone who would punish the innocent priest. This punishment spilled over to the rest of the city, and all the inhabitants were killed. It is amazing how one who was *"hiding himself by the* *baggage"* when he was set to be publicly announced as king (1 Samuel 10:22) could be so transformed after receiving such power.

Of course, the above examples are in addition to the well-known examples of Saul attempting to kill David (1 Samuel 18:10-11, 25; 19:9-11, 15). These were not for any crimes that David had committed but were rooted in Saul's jealousy. He decided that his position gave him the authority to determine that David's life was expendable. Corrupt rulers always disregard the sanctity of human life in one form or another. Saul did this with David, believing that his comfort was worth more than David's life.

Other Examples — The Scriptures are full of examples of human rulers seeking to oppress their fellow man, showing us a clear pattern that such oppression and antagonism toward God-given rights and freedoms is inherent in the institution of civil government.

- **Solomon** — Solomon had been greatly blessed by God in terms of wisdom, peace, and prosperity. Yet this once just king turned to the ways of Saul when he thought his power was threatened. God decided to *"tear the kingdom"* from Solomon and give part of it to Jeroboam (1 Kings 11:11, 29-37). Solomon's reaction was the same as Saul's was to David: *"Solomon sought therefore to put Jeroboam to death; but Jeroboam arose and fled to Egypt to Shishak king of Egypt, and he was in Egypt until the death of Solomon"* (1 Kings 11:40). Jeroboam was appointed by God, and Solomon knew it. Yet the king believed he could reject the will of God and unjustly kill his servant whom God had chosen.
- **Rehoboam** — Solomon's reign ended with the people under heavy taxation. Because of this the

people came to his son, Rehoboam, who had succeeded him with this request: "*Now therefore lighten the hard service of your father and his heavy yoke which he put on us, and we will serve you*" (1 Kings 12:4). Yet Rehoboam foolishly ignored the wisdom of the elders and listened to the young men who served him. He told the people: "*My father made your yoke heavy, but I will add to your yoke; my father disciplined you with whips, but I will discipline you with scorpions*" (1 Kings 12:14). Why did Rehoboam trample on the people's God-given right to the fruits of their labor? Not because of some national security threat or other emergency but simply to exert more power and control over the people.

- **Asa** — For the most part, Asa was a good king (2 Chronicles 14:2-4). Yet even this good king abused his power, oppressed the people, and attacked the God-given right to free speech. When Hanani the seer came to the king and delivered an unfavorable message to him, "*Asa was angry with the seer and put him in prison, for he was enraged at him for this. And Asa oppressed some of the people at the same time*" (2 Chronicles 16:10).

- **The officer at the gate** — When Samaria was under siege, food was scarce, prices were high, and people had even started resorting to cannibalism in order to survive (2 Kings 6:24-29). Elisha prophesied that the siege would end (2 Kings 7:1-2); and God drove out the Arameans, causing them to abandon their camp so quickly that all of their provisions would be left behind (2 Kings 7:5-7). "*So the people went out and plundered the camp of the Arameans. [...] Now the king appointed the royal officer on whose hand he leaned to have charge of the gate; but the people trampled on him at the gate, and he died just as the man of God had said, who spoke when the king came down to him*" (2 Kings

7:16-17). Civil government is to be "*a minster of God... for good*" (Romans 13:4), which does *not* include regulating and restricting one from enjoying the good blessings which God has given. This is exactly why this officer was placed at the gate: to regulate and restrict the flow of people from obtaining the blessings which God had richly given them and that they so desperately needed.

- **Joash** — King Joash and his servants "*conspired against*" Zechariah the son of Jehoiada the priest and "*stoned him to death in the court of the house of the Lord*" (2 Chronicles 24:20-21). What great crime did Zechariah commit? He told the king he had forsaken the Lord and sinned against Him. Thus Zechariah was killed for exercising his natural right of free speech.

The list above of Bible examples is certainly not exhaustive. Besides other examples from the Scriptures, countless examples could be cited from secular history, even from modern times in our own country, showing civil government's chronic history of attacking man's natural rights.

The Difference Between Serving God and Serving the Kingdoms of Men

When Rehoboam and the people "*forsook the law of the Lord*" (2 Chronicles 12:1), Shishak king of Egypt came to fight against him. Shemaiah the prophet revealed God's judgment to Rehoboam: "*You have forsaken Me, so I also have forsaken you to Shishak*" (2 Chronicles 12:5). At this revelation, the king and his princes humbled themselves and repented; but there would still be consequences they would have to suffer.

"When the Lord saw that they humbled themselves, the word of the Lord came to Shemaiah, saying, 'They have humbled themselves so I will not destroy them, but I will grant them some measure of deliverance, and My wrath shall not be poured out on Jerusalem by means of Shishak. But they will become his slaves so that they may learn the difference between My service and the service of the kingdoms of the countries'" (2 Chronicles 12:7-8).

As king, it would be easy for Rehoboam to be unable to relate to the plight of his people under an oppressive ruler. Rehoboam's oppression of the people was the reason why the kingdom was divided and many left from serving him (2 Chronicles 10). But now, under the oppression of Shishak, he would learn what it was like to live under an oppressive king.

"So Shishak king of Egypt came up against Jerusalem, and took the treasures of the house of the Lord and the treasures of the king's palace. He took everything; he even took the golden shields which Solomon had made. Then king Rehoboam made shields of bronze in their place and committed them to the care of the commanders of the guard who guarded the door of the king's house. As often as the king entered the house of the Lord, the guards came and carried them and then brought them back into the guards' room" (2 Chronicles 12:9-11).

Serving an oppressive ruler does not just include obeying the laws of the land. It also includes having your possessions confiscated, settling for inferior replacements, and living in constant fear of those possessions being taken away as well.

Serving the Lord is very different. It includes obedience to His laws (Deuteronomy 11:13-15; Matthew 28:19-20). But instead of the rulers of human kingdoms that pillage the fruits of the people's labor, God provides us with *"every good thing… and every perfect gift"* (James 1:17).

This is the fundamental difference: God gives; government takes. This has been true throughout the history of civil government and will continue to be true until they are all finally destroyed when the Lord returns.

Why is it that civil government so consistently stands against the God-given freedoms of man? We will begin to see the reason for this in the next chapter as we consider the origins of civil government.

3

ORIGINS OF CIVIL GOVERNMENT: A REJECTION OF GOD'S RULE OVER MAN

It is common for brethren to think that God created the institution of civil government. They base this idea on what Paul wrote to the saints in Rome:

> "*Every person is to be in subjection to the governing authorities. For there is no authority except from God, and* **those which exist are established by God**" (Romans 13:1).

A casual reading of this passage can give one the impression that God formed civil government in the beginning. Some even take this so far as to say that *modern* governments have been somehow divinely chosen and that *any* government, no matter how corrupt or wicked, must have been established by God for some purpose. Neither of these ideas are taught in this verse.

First of all, Paul's primary point — the point upon which the rest of his comments about civil government are based — was that God is the supreme authority. He said, "*For there is* **no authority except from God**." Every human ruler is subject to the Lord, just the same as all other men. Those in positions of authority will be held accountable for how they have followed God's standard.

Second, *if* we were to say that this verse is talking about God placing certain rulers and regimes in power by miraculous providence, that does not mean He is still doing this today. Though there is some confusion in the denominational world, brethren generally understand that the age of miracles has ceased because the word of God has been fully revealed (1 Corinthians 13:8-10; Mark 16:19-20). Yet when it comes to human governments, brethren ignore this principle. The Roman Empire played a crucial role in God's plan for His Son to be sacrificed (Acts 2:23) and allow for the rapid spread of the gospel once His kingdom was established (Mark 16:15; Acts 1:8; Colossians 1:23). The Lord does not need to preserve a physical nation as His own peculiar people today; He has a spiritual kingdom (John 18:36). He does not need a certain government in power that will provide favorable conditions in which to establish His kingdom; His kingdom has already been established and will *never* be destroyed (Daniel 2:44). So even if Paul was talking about God placing certain rulers and governments in power, we have no indication in Scripture that this would continue after the fall of Rome.

Third, Paul described God ordaining a *purpose* for government. This will be discussed further in chapter five, but for now let us briefly notice what Paul said about the purpose for which God ordained civil government.

> "*For rulers are not a cause of fear for good behavior, but for evil. Do you want to have no fear of authority? Do what is good and you will have praise from the same; for it is a minister of God to you for good. But if you do what is evil, be afraid; for it does not bear the sword for nothing; for it is a minister of God, an avenger who brings wrath on the one who practices evil*" (Romans 13:3-4).

This is the primary *purpose* of civil government — to punish those who do evil and to support and defend those who practice righteousness. Do all governments fulfill their divinely-given role? Of course not. Throughout history, civil governments have been the greatest source of violent persecution against God's people. So while we certainly understand that not all governments seek to punish evil and defend what is good, Paul said that all governments do have this responsibility from God. Therefore, if God continues to place specific rulers and regimes in power, as many Christians believe, why would He not choose only those who would fulfill *this* purpose? No, civil governments are of man and have been from the beginning. God has simply ordained a specific *purpose* for these governments.

If God did not institute civil government from its beginning, how did it originate? The Scriptures show us that civil government had its origin after the flood with Nimrod.

> *"Now Cush became the father of Nimrod; he became a mighty one on the earth. He was a mighty hunter before the Lord; therefore it is said, 'Like Nimrod a mighty hunter before the Lord.' The beginning of his kingdom was Babel and Erech and Accad and Calneh, in the land of Shinar"* (Genesis 10:8-10).

Nimrod's actions in establishing a kingdom were in rebellion against God. Many people do not (or will not) see this. They read these short verses about Nimrod as simply a benign record of history, rather than **the first great organized rebellion against God since the flood**.

The phrase that is easily overlooked is *"before the Lord."* Nimrod was *"a mighty hunter before the Lord."* He held such a place of prominence among the people that others would use him as a point of comparison — *"Therefore it is said, 'Like Nimrod a mighty hunter before the Lord.'"*

This phrase is often used to mean *in the presence of the Lord* (Genesis 19:27; Exodus 34:34) or *in worship to the Lord* (Exodus 29:11; Deuteronomy 26:10). Because of this, brethren assume that the phrase is used positively here. Yet the word translated *before* (*panim*) has many different uses. In blessing Joseph's sons, Jacob placed "*Ephraim **before** Manasseh*" (Genesis 48:20), meaning he placed Ephraim as chief among Joseph's sons *over* his older brother Manasseh. It is used to describe kings who "***faced** each other*" in battle (2 Kings 14:11). The translators of the New American Standard Bible have also translated this same word as ***against*** (Hosea 5:5; Ezekiel 6:9).

The Bible is not describing anything that Nimrod was doing *in the presence of the Lord* and certainly not *in worship to the Lord*. Rather, it is describing what Nimrod was doing to *place himself before the Lord in the eyes of the people*, making him their chief rather than God. Nimrod was *opposed* to God and wanted the people to forget the Lord and instead look to him as the ultimate authority and the provider of their happiness.

Josephus confirms that Nimrod's actions did not honor God, nor were they innocuous matters that fell into the realm of personal, God-granted liberty. Rather, he acted in rebellion against God.

> "Now it was Nimrod who excited them to such an affront and contempt of God. He was the grandson of Ham, the son of Noah, —a bold man, and of great strength of hand. He persuaded them not to ascribe it to God as if it was through his means they were happy, but to believe that it was their own courage which procured that happiness. He also gradually changed the government into tyranny, —seeing no other way of turning men from the fear of God, but to bring

them into a constant dependence upon his power" (Josephus, *Antiquities*, 1.4.2).

"*The beginning of his kingdom was Babel*" (Genesis 10:10). The fact that Nimrod established Babel (later known as Babylon) is significant for several reasons:

- This was the first man-made civil government. All governments to this point were patriarchal — men were "ruled" by the heads of their households — with the patriarch under the rule of God, not another man.
- Its name means *confusion* (Genesis 11:9) because God used the confusing of their languages to disrupt their rebellious plans.
- The people of God lived in Babylonian captivity for seventy years (2 Chronicles 36:20-21).
- The Babylonians not only besieged Jerusalem, enslaved the people, and broke down the city walls, they also burned down the city, including the house of the Lord (2 Kings 25:8-12).
- Babylon was the first world empire in Daniel's prophecy. It would be followed by the Medo-Persian, Greek, and Roman empires (Daniel 2:36-43).
- In the book of Revelation, the Roman authorities who had killed Jesus and many other martyrs are described as Babylon: "*Babylon the great, the mother of harlots and of the abominations of the earth*" (Revelation 17:5).

It is important that we understand this fact. God did not institute civil government. Rather, civil government was created in opposition to God by those who rebelled against Him. In establishing his kingdom, Nimrod supplanted God and ruled over the people. The beginnings of civil government were not by God's institution but came as a result of man's rebellion against God.

This theme is continued throughout the Old Testament. The descendants of Abraham were ruled by God Himself. When they came into the promised land, they were to destroy the inhabitants of the land. They were not to make any treaty or intermarry with them. They were to be a *separate* people (Deuteronomy 7:1-6). Some time later after they had conquered the land of Canaan, they demanded a king patterned after the governments of the nations around them. This was seen as a rejection of God's rule over them (1 Samuel 8:7).

This history is important. While we are not under the same covenant today (Colossians 2:14; Hebrews 8:8), we need to remember the lessons contained in these passages. But even though God did not *establish* civil government, since man was determined to use it, He *ordained* it for a particular purpose. This will be discussed further in chapter five.

But before we discuss what God ordained with respect to civil government, we need to consider what a God-ordered society looks like. To do this, we will see what God commanded the children of Israel after He delivered them from Egypt. The foundation of the law that was handed down to the new nation of Israel at Mount Sinai shows us the foundation of any godly society.

4

THE FOUNDATION FOR A GODLY SOCIETY

"Then God spoke all these words, saying, 'I am the Lord your God, who brought you out of the land of Egypt, out of the house of slavery.'

"'You shall have no other gods before Me.'

"'You shall not make for yourselves an idol, or any likeness of what is in heaven above or on the earth beneath or in the water under the earth. You shall not worship them or serve them; for I, the Lord your God, am a jealous God, visiting the iniquity of the fathers on the children, on the third and the fourth generations of those who hate Me, but showing lovingkindness to thousands, to those who love Me and keep My commandments.'

"'You shall not take the name of the Lord your God in vain, for the Lord will not leave him unpunished who takes His name in vain.'

"'Remember the sabbath day, to keep it holy. Six days you shall labor and do all your work, but the seventh day is a sabbath of the Lord your God; in it you shall not do any work, you or your son or your daughter, your male or your female servant or your cattle or your

sojourner who stays with you. For in six days the Lord made the heavens and the earth, the sea and all that is in them, and rested on the seventh day; therefore the Lord blessed the sabbath day and made it holy.'

"'Honor your father and your mother, that your days may be prolonged in the land which the Lord your God gives you.'

"'You shall not murder.'

"'You shall not commit adultery.'

"'You shall not steal.'

"'You shall not bear false witness against your neighbor.'

"'You shall not covet your neighbor's house; you shall not covet your neighbor's wife or his male servant or his female servant or his ox or his donkey or anything that belongs to your neighbor'" (Exodus 20:1-17).

The Ten Commandments — the laws engraved onto stone which God delivered to Moses for the children of Israel — give us the blueprint for the foundation of any godly or righteous society. These Ten Commandments are regularly assaulted by those on the "left" as having no place in our government or our schools. The stated reason for their opposition is that the Ten Commandments represent a religious element that has no place in anything related to government. Yet the Ten Commandments represent more than just religion. The reason there is such strong opposition to the display of the Ten Commandments by the "left" is because the Ten Commandments stand in direct opposition to the Liberal's ideal for society.

Many today view the Ten Commandments as part of the foundation of our religion. Yet they are part of the Old Law which was nailed to the cross (Colossians 2:14). Does this mean they are of no value for us today? Certainly not! But we must use them properly. The Old Testament was written and is preserved "*for our instruction*" (Romans 15:4). When we study the Ten Commandments, we find the foundations of a godly society.

The giving of the Ten Commandments marked the first time when God's people were joined together as a *nation*. This is significant. Nations (kingdoms) did not have a favorable beginning with the Lord (as discussed in the previous chapter). God's people had lived *among* the nations but did not form together as their own. This was the time of the patriarchs.

But here, as the children of Israel assembled at Mount Sinai, God's people would be assembled as a nation. This was part of God's plan. He told the patriarch Abram, "*I will make you a great nation*" (Genesis 12:2). God did this on His terms.

The wise man wrote, "*Righteousness exalts a nation, but sin is a disgrace to any people*" (Proverbs 14:34). God shows the framework for a righteous nation here in the Ten Commandments.

Why Should We Study This Today?

Why is it important to study how the Ten Commandments provide the basis for a godly society? We are not under this law today (Colossians 2:14; Hebrews 8:8-9). Furthermore, there is not one nation that has been designated as God's chosen people today. His people make up a *spiritual* kingdom (John 18:36).

Yet these commandments are inspired and are profitable to us (2 Timothy 3:16; Romans 15:4) even if the law has changed. Many of the Ten Commandments are also repeated in the New

Testament, so it reinforces our current law. But there is also a very clear and diligent effort underway to fix our country. If we want to take advantage of opportunities to show people the wisdom of God in order to hopefully lead them to a greater interest in the truth, this is an excellent place to start.

It is important to note that the Ten Commandments are not directed to or about the government — they are to the individual. That means that each one of us and all those we may teach can make personal application from these truths.

How do we fix a broken society? It will not come through government policy but with the people's change of heart. In the Ten Commandments, we are taught about one's relationship with God and with others and also the type of character which one ought to have. The framework for a godly and righteous society does not start with government. In fact, if all people would follow these commands, government would be unnecessary. Notice what Paul wrote:

> "For this, 'You shall not commit adultery, you shall not murder, you shall not steal, you shall not covet,' and if there is any other commandment, it is summed up in this saying, 'You shall love your neighbor as yourself.' Love does no wrong to a neighbor; therefore love is the fulfillment of the law" (Romans 13:9-10).

This comes immediately after what Paul revealed about the divinely ordained role of civil government. He mentioned a few of the Ten Commandments and said they all have one thing in common — love. Love is the fulfillment of the Law. This means that if everyone exercised love properly toward one another, there would be no God-given purpose for civil government, thus making it irrelevant and unnecessary.

When the Ten Commandments were given, God spoke directly to the people (Exodus 20:1). Before this, Moses was used as God's spokesman. Afterward, Moses again spoke to the people for God (Exodus 20:19). But in giving the Ten Commandments, God addressed the people directly. All of the laws that would later be given were based upon this framework. It was important for the people to understand that God was the Lawgiver. It is important for us as well to understand that these commands came from God.

Preface to the Ten Commandments

"I am the Lord your God, who brought you out of the land of Egypt, out of the house of slavery" (Exodus 20:2).

God began the revelation of His law by telling the people, *"I am the Lord your God."* He was the ultimate authority. Though He was not discussing civil government in this context, Paul would later remind his audience of an important truth for understanding our place before civil authority. The apostle told the saints in Rome, *"For there is no authority except from God"* (Romans 13:1). Government or no government, we are accountable to the Lord.

The Israelites lived under a *theocracy*. God was their King and His commandments to them not only included spiritual law but also civil law. We do not live under a government today which has God as its head. But He is still the primary authority over us. Peter showed us this in his answer to the counsel that threatened him for preaching Christ against their orders. When divine law conflicts with human law, we must answer as Peter did: *"We must obey God rather than men"* (Acts 5:29).

It is important to note that the Ten Commandments, the foundation for a godly society, though they were given to the nation as a whole, were directed toward the individual. God said, *"I am the Lord your God, who brought you out of the land of Egypt."* For a society to function as God intends for it to, it requires *individuals* recognizing their accountability before God and exercising *personal responsibility*. Without this, any effort to fix the problems in our country will ultimately be in vain.

At the beginning, God also reminded the Israelites of the fact that He brought them out of the house of slavery in Egypt. God wants people to be free, as we have seen in a previous chapter. But this freedom must be used in His service. After discussing civil authorities, Peter wrote, *"Act as free men, and do not use your freedom as a covering for evil, but use it as bondslaves of God"* (1 Peter 2:16). This need for obedience is evident in the fact that God cited their deliverance from bondage and then immediately proceeded to give them these commandments.

I: No Other Gods

"You shall have no other gods before Me" (Exodus 20:3).

Remember the preface to these commandments. The Ten Commandments were given after the Israelites were delivered from bondage in *Egypt*. The Egyptians believed in *many* gods. Pharaoh was seen by the Egyptians *as a god*. He was the one who stood between the gods and the people.

For a society to function as it ought, the people must serve the one, true God exclusively. This point was made in the command about idols: *"You shall not worship them or serve them; for I, the Lord your God, am a jealous God"* (Exodus 20:5). This does not mean that a godly society today should attempt to establish a theocracy as existed at the birth of the nation of Israel. Again, these commandments were directed toward *individuals*, not a governing body. A society functions at its best when people have made the choice to worship and serve the Lord.

With Egypt, there was also a connection between false gods and civil government. Pharaoh, the head of the government, was a god or represented the gods. The Bible also speaks of other heads of government who were elevated in the eyes of the people to the status of a god. One in particular was Herod. When he spoke, the people would cry out, *"The voice of a god and not of a man!"* (Acts 12:22). Government has a divine purpose (this will be discussed in the next chapter). But when civil government — either the institution as a whole or an individual (such as a king) — steps between man and God, there will be problems.

God's ideal for society is one in which the people have the freedom to choose to serve Him *and* make the choice to do so. If civil authorities exist in an ideal society, they will allow the people the freedom to worship. Individuals would then worship the one, true God. Governments might restrict the God-given freedom to worship, and individuals may worship God anyway (and are expected to do so — Acts 5:29). Governments might also allow the freedom to worship and individuals choose to *not* worship or choose to worship a false God. But societies function best when you have both elements: men worshiping and serving God without government interference.

Furthermore, it is significant that this commandment is *first* among those that were given. This means that as we serve God, He must take precedence over everything. Pleasing Him is more important than pleasing the civil authorities, our friends and family, and even ourselves. None of the other commandments matter if we do not put the Lord first in all things.

II: No Idols

"You shall not make for yourselves an idol, or any likeness of what is in heaven above or on the earth beneath or in the water under the earth. You shall not worship them or serve them; for I, the Lord your God, am a jealous God, visiting the iniquity of the fathers on the children, on the third and the fourth generations of those who hate Me, but showing lovingkindness to thousands, to those who love Me and keep My commandments" (Exodus 20:4-6).

When we think of idols (graven images), we tend to think of the false gods of the nations around the children of Israel. The Israelites were certainly prohibited from worshiping these "gods," but this prohibition is addressed in the first commandment. The prohibition against idols is something different. It is not limited to false gods but would also prohibit making an idol of the one, true God. When you read the instructions regarding the tabernacle and the furniture that was to go with it, there is no mention of any physical representation of God. All graven images, whether meant to depict a false god or the true God, were prohibited.

What is an idol or a graven image? It is a creation of man, crafted by him and comprised of things which God has created. God mocked this practice of idolatry.

"Surely he cuts cedars for himself, and takes a cypress or an oak and raises it for himself among the trees of the forest. He plants a fir, and the rain makes it grow. Then it becomes something for a man to burn, so he takes one of them and warms himself; he also makes a fire to bake bread. He also makes a god and worships it; he makes it a graven image and falls down before it. Half of it he burns in the fire; over this half he eats meat as he roasts

a roast and is satisfied. He also warms himself and says, 'Aha! I am warm, I have seen the fire.' But the rest of it he makes into a god, his graven image. He falls down before it and worships; he also prays to it and says, 'Deliver me, for you are my god'" (Isaiah 44:14-17).

Why was idolatry condemned? And why is it relevant to our study here? One of the lessons from this commandment is that we need to believe in something that is *unseen*. This is what the Bible describes as *faith*.

> *"Now faith is the assurance of things hoped for, the conviction of things not seen"* (Hebrews 11:1).

> *"For we walk by faith, not by sight"* (2 Corinthians 5:7).

The Israelites, without Moses, thought they needed something tangible to make God seem real to them. So in his absence, they made a golden calf (Exodus 32:1). While this was an idol, it was not a false god. It was meant to represent the one, true God. When the calf was made, Aaron said, *"This is your god, O Israel, who brought you up from the land of Egypt!"* (Exodus 32:8). Even though this was meant to represent the God who *"brought* [them] *out of the land of Egypt"* (Exodus 20:1), it made God want to destroy them (Exodus 32:9-10).

Jesus told us, *"God is spirit"* (John 4:24). The greatest blessings He bestows upon us are *spiritual* (Ephesians 1:3-14). His reward for us is eternal (Romans 6:23). If we focus on the lesser things, we will be doomed to fail. Paul wrote, *"For the mind set on the flesh is death, but the mind set on the Spirit is life and peace"* (Romans 8:6). We certainly have responsibilities in this life, but we must remember that there is more to our existence than the things of this life.

If the people of a nation do not have faith in something unseen but only believe in what they can see, hear, and touch for themselves, there is no motivation to be good and treat others as they ought to treat them.

III: Do Not Take God's Name in Vain

"You shall not take the name of the Lord your God in vain, for the Lord will not leave him unpunished who takes His name in vain" (Exodus 20:7).

This refers to one invoking God's name carelessly or irreverently. The underlying principle behind this commandment is that man must have a respect and reverence for God. The first two commandments show us that the Israelites were to have no other gods and have faith in the unseen. This commandment builds upon the first two: the one, true God whom we acknowledge in faith must be respected by man.

Respecting God is important, particularly when it comes to how the people of a society function with one another. If we respect God, we will do certain things:

1. We will listen to Him.
2. We will obey Him.
3. We will make decisions according to His revealed principles.

If people have enough respect for God that they listen to Him, obey Him, and consult His word whenever a question arises about a proper course of action, society will function better. When people do not respect God, and therefore do not obey God, society falls apart. This should become clear to us as we look at the remaining commandments.

IV: Remember the Sabbath

"Remember the sabbath day, to keep it holy. Six days you shall labor and do all your work, but the seventh day is a sabbath of the Lord your God; in it you shall not do any work, you or your son or your daughter, your male or your female servant or your cattle or your sojourner who stays with you. For in six days the Lord made the heavens and the earth, the sea and all that is in them, and rested on the seventh day; therefore the Lord blessed the sabbath day and made it holy" (Exodus 20:8-11).

The Sabbath law was not carried over into the New Testament. Therefore, it is not a religious requirement for Christians today. It was given specifically to the Jewish people (Exodus 31:13-17). Yet the commandment to remember the Sabbath day contains some principles that are important for us to remember. These principles, when accepted by the people of a society, will be a great source of strength to the society.

The first principle we will consider has to do with the reason for the commandment. Why were the Israelites to remember the Sabbath day and keep it holy? Remember that this day was meant to correspond to a significant event — the Creation.

"For in six days the Lord made the heavens and the earth, the sea and all that is in them, and rested on the seventh day; therefore the Lord blessed the sabbath day and made it holy" (Exodus 20:11).

The Sabbath was not just for giving the people a break from their work. It was meant to remind people of God's work in Creation, followed by His rest on the seventh day. There are several important reminders from the Creation about God and ourselves.

- *"In the beginning God created the heavens and the earth"* (Genesis 1:1). This reminds us that He exists since a design demands a designer (cf. Hebrews 3:4). The fact that He was able to create something from nothing also shows us *"His eternal power"* (Romans 1:20).
- The creation also shows that He cares for us. *"Then God said, 'Behold, I have given you every plant yielding seed that is on the surface of all the earth, and every tree which has fruit yielding seed; it shall be food for you; and to every beast of the earth and to every bird of the sky and to every thing that moves on the earth which has life, I have given every green plant for food'; and it was so. God saw all that He had made, and behold, it was very good"* (Genesis 1:29-31). God has provided everything we need to survive and prosper through the things which He has created.
- Knowing that God is our Creator reminds us that we are not the product of some great cosmic accident. We are here because it was God's will for us to be here (Revelation 4:11).
- The understanding that God deliberately placed man on the earth and that we are not the product of random chance tells us that we have a purpose in this life. The wise man succinctly explained this purpose: *"The conclusion, when all has been heard, is: fear God and keep His commandments, because this applies to every person"* (Ecclesiastes 12:13).

Understanding that God is our Creator ought to lead us to obey Him as the wise man pointed out in the verse above. When a society is made up of people who remember that God is their Creator and that everything they enjoy in this life is here by His providence, that society will function as God intends for it to function.

The second principle derived from the Sabbath law that is needed for a godly society is that men must be hardworking. The Sabbath law mandated rest on the seventh day following six days of labor. It is interesting that in our current culture, the norm is for people to work not six but *five* days a week. This seems like such a burden to many that they cannot bear the thought of giving up their "weekend" for work. Sadly, many others do not want to work at all and take advantage of friends, family, or government programs to keep from working. Yet under this law, the Israelites had to be told, under penalty of death (Exodus 31:14-15), not to work on the seventh day of the week. How many people today complain about working just five days a week (not counting holidays, vacations, sick time, etc.)?

This is not to say that it is wrong for someone to work only five days a week. Our economy is different. Technology is more advanced. Many people are able to live comfortably with a forty hour work week. But the point is that God intends for society to be made up of hardworking people. This characteristic is commended, not only here but throughout the Bible:

> *"Go to the ant, O sluggard, observe her ways and be wise, which, having no chief, officer or ruler, prepares her food in the summer and gathers her provision in the harvest"* (Proverbs 6:6-8).

> *"For you yourselves know how you ought to follow our example, because we did not act in an undisciplined manner among you, nor did we eat anyone's bread without paying for it, but with labor and hardship we kept working night and day so that we would not be a burden to any of you; not because we do not have the right to this, but in order to offer ourselves as a model for*

*you, so that you would follow our example. For even
when we were with you, we used to give you this order:
if anyone is not willing to work, then he is not to eat,
either"* (2 Thessalonians 3:7-10).

Lately our society has been infected with a slothful mentality that causes one to believe he is entitled to the fruits of labor without actually laboring for himself. Having people who are willing to work hard to provide for themselves will have a great, positive impact on society as a whole.

V: Honor Your Father and Mother

*"Honor your father and your mother, that your days
may be prolonged in the land which the Lord your God
gives you"* (Exodus 20:12).

This commandment is repeated in the New Testament, and Paul said it was *"the first commandment with a promise"* (Ephesians 6:2). This promise — that their days would be prolonged in the land — was about life, prosperity, and security. Generally, one who honors his father and mother will receive such a benefit. Why? Parents want what is best for their children, and they have wisdom (both in the form of instruction and personal experience) to pass on to their children. Therefore, it is good for children to honor their parents.

This commandment specifically mentions the responsibility of the younger generation to obey their parents. But there is a broader principle here as well that the younger generation must respect the older generation. This means that this commandment carries responsibilities past childhood and into one's adult life. Jesus explained this during one of His confrontations with the Pharisees and scribes.

> *"And He answered and said to them, 'Why do you yourselves transgress the commandment of God for the sake of your tradition? For God said, "Honor your father and mother," and, "He who speaks evil of father or mother is to be put to death." But you say, "Whoever says to his father or mother, 'Whatever I have that would help you has been given to God,' he is not to honor his father or his mother," And by this you invalidated the word of God for the sake of your tradition"'* (Matthew 15:3-6).

This command clearly applied to adults as well since Jesus indicted these grown men of transgressing it. The Pharisees and scribes were condemned because they refused to care for their parents' needs in their old age. The Scriptures are clear that children have the primary responsibility of caring for their parents later in life.

> *"Honor widows who are widows indeed; but if any widow has children or grandchildren, they must first learn to practice piety in regard to their own family and to make some return to their parents; for this is acceptable in the sight of God"* (1 Timothy 5:3-4).

Paul said that widows who met certain qualifications *and* had no one to care for them could be helped by the church (1 Timothy 5:5-16). But if there was family who could care for a certain widow, the family was to do it; and *"the church must not be burdened, so that it may assist those who are widows indeed"* (1 Timothy 5:16).

In our society, it has become expected that the government ought to take care of needy parents rather than their children. Costs for programs that provide aid for seniors continue to rise and, if not corrected, will bankrupt the country. Older citizens surely need to be cared for. How is this to be done? First of all, the Scriptures show us the responsibility for each of us to provide for ourselves, not just so we will not be in need, but so that we will have something to pass down to our children and grandchildren.

> "*Here for this third time I am ready to come to you, and I will not be a burden to you; for I do not seek what is yours, but you; for children are not responsible to save up for their parents, but parents for their children*" (2 Corinthians 12:14).

> "*A good man leaves an inheritance to his children's children, and the wealth of the sinner is stored up for the righteous*" (Proverbs 13:22).

Though this may be a worthy goal, we all understand that life does not always turn out in the way we plan for it. As a result, even godly people who do their best may find themselves needing help in their older years. The responsibility to care for these individuals falls to their families. A lot of problems in our society would be solved if parents worked diligently to make provisions for themselves and children stepped up to fill in anything that lacked. Jesus taught that this was how one honors his parents.

There is another lesson that is implied in this command about the responsibility of the older generation. They are to cause their children to honor them — not by force, but by discipline and teaching.

> "*Fathers, do not provoke your children to anger, but bring them up in the discipline and instruction of the Lord*" (Ephesians 6:4).

> "*Furthermore, we had earthly fathers to discipline us, and we respected them; shall we not much rather be*

subject to the Father of spirits, and live?" (Hebrews 12:9).

"These words, which I am commanding you today, shall be on your heart. You shall teach them diligently to your sons and shall talk of them when you sit in your house and when you walk by the way and when you lie down and when you rise up" (Deuteronomy 6:6-7).

"Train up a child in the way he should go, even when he is old he will not depart from it" (Proverbs 22:6).

Parents must teach their children so they learn the truth, discipline their children so they learn respect, and show themselves to be examples lest their hypocrisy tells the children that following God's will is unimportant. Failure to do these things will result in a generation like the one that followed Joshua's generation.

"All that generation also were gathered to their fathers; and there arose another generation after them who did not know the Lord, nor yet the work which He had done for Israel. Then the sons of Israel did evil in the sight of the Lord and served the Baals, and they forsook the Lord, the God of their fathers, who had brought them out of the land of Egypt, and followed other gods from among the gods of the peoples who were among them, and bowed themselves down to them; thus they provoked the Lord to anger" (Judges 2:10-12).

The commandment to honor one's parents has a greater impact than just over one family. It will affect how each generation respects and serves God.

VI: Do Not Murder

"You shall not murder" (Exodus 20:13).

There is a little bit of confusion over the translation in the King James Version of this verse: *"Thou shalt not kill."* This has led some to conclude that all instances of one man taking another man's life is condemned (including capital punishment). Yet this verse does not prohibit all killing.

- Capital punishment was permitted under the Law (Exodus 21:12; Leviticus 24:17; Numbers 15:35).
- Accidentally taking someone's life was not a capital crime (Numbers 35:10-12, 22-25).
- Self-defense was allowed under the Law (Exodus 22:2).

From the above examples, we can see that this commandment is specifically about *murder*. The command against murder was carried over into the New Testament as well (Romans 1:29; 13:9; 1 Timothy 1:9), and no precept was handed down from above that would broaden the definition of *killing* beyond *murder*.

This commandment is important for any society to function as God intends for it to function, not just to keep citizens from murdering their fellowman, but for the broader principle upon which this command is based. The prohibition of murder is grounded in a necessary respect for the sanctity of human life.

All men have been made in the image of God (Genesis 1:26-27). For this reason, murder was condemned; and capital punishment was to be used against those who commit such a crime. *"Whoever sheds man's blood, by man his blood shall be shed, for in the image of God He made man"* (Genesis 9:6). Because all men are made in the image of God, we must love one another.

> *"For this is the message which you have heard from the beginning, that we should love one another; not as Cain, who was of the evil one and slew his brother. And for what reason did he slay him? Because his deeds were evil, and his brother's were righteous"* (1 John 3:11-12).

As we have already seen, love is the basis for all of these commandments. Paul wrote, *"Owe nothing to anyone except to love one another; for he who loves his neighbor has fulfilled the law. For this, 'You shall not commit adultery, you shall not murder, you shall not steal, you shall not covet,' and if there is any other commandment, it is summed up in this saying, 'You shall love your neighbor as yourself.' Love does no wrong to a neighbor; therefore love is the fulfillment of the law"* (Romans 13:8-10). Because of our love for our others, we are not to bring about harm to them.

When discussing this, especially as it pertains to the foundation of society, a question will arise about abortion. Most understand that murder is wrong. But does abortion count? The Scriptures teach that abortion most certainly does count as murder. Notice the following passages:

> *"If men struggle with each other and strike a woman with child so that she gives birth prematurely, yet there is no injury, he shall surely be fined as the woman's husband may demand of him, and he shall pay as the judges decide. But if there is any further injury, then you shall appoint as a penalty life for life, eye for eye, tooth for tooth, hand for hand, foot for foot, burn for burn, wound for wound, bruise for bruise"* (Exodus 21:22-25).

The same Law that condemned murder imposed the same penalty on harming an unborn child as one who was already born. Furthermore, the Bible shows us that God sees an unborn child as a unique individual, rather than just a mass of tissue.

> *"For You formed my inward parts; You wove me in my mother's womb. I will give thanks to You, for I am fearfully and wonderfully made; wonderful are Your works, and my soul knows it very well. My frame was not hidden from You, when I was made in secret, and skillfully wrought in the depths of the earth; Your eyes have seen my unformed substance; and in Your book were written the days that were ordained for me, when as yet there was not one of them"* (Psalm 139:13-16).

> *"Before I formed you in the womb I knew you, and before you were born I consecrated you; I have appointed you a prophet to the nations"* (Jeremiah 1:5).

The Scriptures show us that there is no difference between a born child and an unborn child. Notice two verses:

> *"When Elizabeth heard Mary's greeting, the **baby** leaped in her womb; and Elizabeth was filled with the Holy Spirit"* (Luke 1:41).

> *"This will be a sign for you: you will find a **baby** wrapped in cloths and lying in a manger"* (Luke 2:12).

The first verse describes John in the womb. The second verse speaks of Jesus after He was born. Both the unborn John and the newly born Jesus were called by the same term — baby (Greek: *brephos*). Those who argue for abortion are calling for the killing of a life that the Holy Spirit calls the same as the life of one who has already been born. The issue of abortion is not a matter of liberty and a woman having the right over her own body. It is about protecting the life of an unborn child who has been made in the image of God. A society that is founded on godly principles will protect this life, not condone or fund the extermination of those who have been deemed to be too inconvenient.

Euthanasia is another question that has arisen in our society. It is sometimes called "mercy killing" and is usually advocated in order to end the life of one who is in chronic ill health. Is such a practice good and acceptable for a society that is founded upon godly principles? The Scriptures give us the answer: no, it is not.

When Saul was badly wounded in battle, he took his own life to prevent the Philistines from capturing him alive (1 Samuel 31:3-4). After this, a young man came to David to inform him of Saul's death and to bring him the king's crown and bracelet (2 Samuel 1:2-4, 10). When David questioned him, this young man lied about what had happened.

> "*The young man who told him said, 'By chance I happened to be on Mount Gilboa, and behold, Saul was leaning on his spear. And behold, the chariots and the horsemen pursued him closely. When he looked behind him, he saw me and called to me. And I said, "Here I am," He said to me, "Who are you?" And I answered him, "I am an Amalekite." Then he said to me, "Please stand beside me and kill me, for agony has seized me because my life still lingers in me." So I stood beside him and killed him, because I knew that he could not live after he had fallen. And I took the crown which was on his head and the bracelet which was on his arm, and I have brought them here to my lord'*" (2 Samuel 1:6-10).

The Scriptures reveal to us that Saul fell on his own sword. This man lied and said that he killed Saul at his request. David was forced to make a judgment based upon this man's word.

What the young man described was a "mercy killing." How did David, a man after God's own heart (Acts 13:22), react?

> "*Then David said to him, 'How is it you were not afraid to stretch out your hand to destroy the Lord's anointed?' And David called one of the young men and said, 'Go, cut him down.' So he struck him and he died. David said to him, 'Your blood is on your head, for your mouth has testified against you, saying, "I have killed the Lord's anointed"'*" (2 Samuel 1:14-16).

By testifying (falsely) that he killed a mortally wounded Saul, this man admitted to murdering the king and was worthy of capital punishment.

The Scriptures teach that those who are older are to be respected. As we have already noticed, the command to honor one's father and mother applied even after the children were grown.

> "*You shall rise up before the grayheaded and honor the aged, and you shall revere your God; I am the Lord*" (Leviticus 19:32).

Respect for one's elders is tied to respect for God. Those who are of the older generation are to be honored, not have their lives ended when it becomes more convenient for the younger generation to do so.

VII: Do Not Commit Adultery

> "*You shall not commit adultery*" (Exodus 20:14).

The prohibition of adultery shows the obvious need for personal morality and purity in the realm of sexual activity. The law of Moses condemned various forms of *fornication*, including incest (Leviticus 18:6-17), adultery (Leviticus 18:20), homosexuality (Leviticus 18:22), and bestiality (Leviticus 18:23). The New Testament law also condemns fornication generally (1 Corinthians 6:18; 1 Thessalonians 4:3), as well as adultery and homosexuality specifically (1 Corinthians 6:9).

Yet when we consider this from the standpoint of our study about how the Ten Commandments provide the foundation for a godly society, it is significant that the seventh commandment condemns *adultery* specifically, not the general category of *fornication* (which would be dealt with at various times in the giving of the Law).

The fact that God's foundation of society condemns adultery shows the importance of honoring the institution of marriage.

> *"Marriage is to be held in honor among all, and the marriage bed is to be undefiled; for fornicators and adulterers God will judge"* (Hebrews 13:4).

It is important to note that God intends for marriage to be honored *"among all."* He created the institution of marriage in the beginning with Adam and Eve (Genesis 2:24). Jesus appealed to this establishment of marriage when He explained the truth about divorce (Matthew 19:4-6). Marriage is not merely a cultural matter, but is an institution that was given to man, having its origins in the mind of God.

Marriage is important because it gives one a companion and partner in a stable relationship. God saw the loneliness of Adam and gave him the perfect gift to address it — Eve.

> *"Then the Lord God said, 'It is not good for the man to be alone; I will make him a helper suitable for him'"* (Genesis 2:18).

God, the great power behind Creation, was able to give Adam whatever it was he needed to fill the void in his life on the earth. None of the animals would provide sufficient companionship and help to Adam (Genesis 2:19-20). So God had to create a companion and help meet. He made "*a woman*" (Genesis 2:22), not another man. In God's institution of marriage, the man and woman have different, complementary roles to play (Ephesians 5:22-33).

Knowing that the man and woman have different roles in marriage that perfectly complement one another and that all of this is by God's design, it is no wonder that the Hebrew writer said, "*Marriage is to be held in honor among all*" (Hebrews 13:4).

But the Hebrew writer made an additional point. Not only is marriage to be honored, but "*the marriage bed is to be undefiled*" (Hebrews 13:4). It surprises no one when defiling the marriage bed (*adultery*) leads to divorce. Jesus even gave this as the sole cause that would give one divine permission to put away his spouse (Matthew 19:9). Obviously, divorces happen for other reasons as well; but Jesus said, "*Because of your hardness of heart Moses permitted you to divorce your wives;* **but from the beginning it has not been this way**" (Matthew 19:8). From the beginning, God intended marriage to be a *lifelong* relationship between a man and a woman.

Divorce is a huge problem in our society. Besides this, there are many who do not understand or respect the fact that God designed marriage to be the relationship in which one can lawfully fulfill sexual desires (Matthew 19:6; Hebrews 13:4). Because of this, they engage in sexual activity before and without marriage which results in homes with single mothers where the father is nowhere to be found.

It is easy to see, both through statistics and by our own observation, that those in broken homes are at a disadvantage compared to those in stable, two-parent households. Many unsustainable, failing government programs have been introduced in order to try to help those in these unfortunate circumstances. While we understand that there will always be some single-parent households (if for no other reason than for the death of one of the parents), many problems in society (poverty, crime, drug abuse, etc.) would be significantly reduced if people would develop a proper respect for the institution of marriage and hold it "*in honor*" as God expects.

VIII: Do Not Steal

"*You shall not steal*" (Exodus 20:15).

There are some principles contained in this command that, if followed, will make for a better society.

The reason why stealing was prohibited was because man had a right to his own property. This principle has been expressed several times in Scripture.

> "*Here is what I have seen to be good and fitting: to eat, to drink and enjoy oneself in all one's labor in which he toils under the sun during the few years of his life which God has given him; for this is his reward. Furthermore, as for every man to whom God has given riches and wealth, He has also empowered him to eat from them and to receive his reward and rejoice in his labor; this is the gift of God*" (Ecclesiastes 5:18-19).

> "*But he answered and said to one of them, 'Friend, I am doing you no wrong; did you not agree with me for a denarius? Take what is yours and go, but I wish to give to this last man the same as to you. Is it not lawful for me to do what I wish with what is my own? Or is your*

eye envious because I am generous?"' (Matthew 20:13-15).

"While it remained unsold, did it not remain your own? And after it was sold, was it not under your control? Why is it that you have conceived this deed in your heart? You have not lied to men but to God" (Acts 5:4).

These verses show us that each one has the divine right to use his own possessions as he sees fit. The blessings that we have come from God (Ecclesiastes 5:18; James 1:17). Therefore, the blessings that others receive come from God as well. We have no right to take from others by force. To do this demonstrates a lack of love for our fellow man (cf. Romans 13:9-10).

We need to remember to look for our blessings that come from God, not the blessings He has give to others (cf. Exodus 20:17). Stealing not only shows a lack of respect for others but a lack of respect for God who blessed us in the way that He has. Paul teaches us that we must learn *"to be content in whatever circumstances"* we find ourselves, whether our circumstances are humble or prosperous (Philippians 4:11-12).

The punishments listed for stealing reinforce the point that personal property rights were to be respected, for punishment focused on restitution.

"If a man steals an ox or a sheep and slaughters it or sells it, he shall pay five oxen for the ox and four sheep for the sheep. If the thief is caught while breaking in and is struck so that he dies, there will be no bloodguiltiness on his account. But if the sun has risen on him, there will be bloodguiltiness on his account. He shall surely make restitution; if he owns nothing, then he shall be sold for his theft. If what he stole is actually

found alive in his possession, whether an ox or a donkey or a sheep, he shall pay double" (Exodus 22:1-4).

If one was caught stealing, he did not go to jail where he would be housed, clothed, fed, given time to exercise, etc. Interestingly, there was no jail time given as punishment under the Law of Moses. Instead, the thief would make *restitution.* The punishment was to be more than just a deterrent, it was meant to make things right with the victim of the crime. This would deter those who would steal simply to avoid working for themselves because when they were caught, they would have to work even harder for someone else.

This commandment also emphasizes personal responsibility. A man is to work to provide for himself rather than take the fruits of another man's labor. God's plan is for the one who is blessed to enjoy his blessings.

> *"Furthermore, as for every man to whom God has given riches and wealth, He has also empowered him to eat from them and to receive his reward and rejoice in his labor; this is the gift of God"* (Ecclesiastes 5:19).

Rather than looking at what others possess, one who is able-bodied must work to provide for himself and his family and to be able to help those who are in need.

> *"For even when we were with you, we used to give you this order: if anyone is not willing to work, then he is not to eat, either"* (2 Thessalonians 3:10).

> *"But if anyone does not provide for his own, and especially for those of his household, he has denied the faith and is worse than an unbeliever"* (1 Timothy 5:8).

> *"He who steals must steal no longer; but rather he must labor, performing with his own hands what is good, so that he will have something to share with one who has need"* (Ephesians 4:28).

Our society is facing certain difficulties because a substantial number of people believe they are somehow entitled to the fruits of another man's labor. Not all of those who believe this will steal from others (though some certainly will); but they are perfectly content to call for the use of government force to confiscate and redistribute the wealth of others. When the able-bodied refuse to work for themselves and want to live off of the labors of others, society is in trouble. We must exercise personal responsibility in providing for ourselves.

IX: Do Not Bear False Witness

> *"You shall not bear false witness against your neighbor"* (Exodus 20:16).

Two points are emphasized in this commandment that are essential to society: truth and justice. Regarding the first of these, truth, Paul told the brethren in Thessalonica that we must love the truth (2 Thessalonians 2:10). The wise man spoke of the value of truth when he said, *"Buy truth, and do not sell it, get wisdom and instruction and understanding"* (Proverbs 23:23). Loving and valuing the truth is a necessary component for a society to function as God designed.

> *"These are the things which you should do: speak the truth to one another; judge with truth and judgment for peace in your gates"* (Zechariah 8:16).

The commandment against bearing false witness is more than just a prohibition of lying. It is about *justice.* People today sometimes talk about "social justice." This type of justice is not based upon truth but upon man's subjective and misguided concept of fairness. But the prophet said that judgments must be made based upon *truth*. The poor were not to be oppressed (Zechariah 7:9-10) nor were they to be shown partiality over others when judgments were being made (Exodus 23:3). An objective standard of truth is the only fair and right basis for justice.

> *"A king who sits on the throne of justice disperses all evil with his eyes"* (Proverbs 20:8).

Justice must exist for a society to function properly. But in order for justice to be done, as important as it is for authorities to work for it, each citizen has a responsibility to carry out as well.

> *"You shall not bear a false report; do not join your hand with a wicked man to be a malicious witness. You shall not follow the masses in doing evil, nor shall you testify in a dispute so as to turn aside after a multitude in order to pervert justice; nor shall you be partial to a poor man in his dispute"* (Exodus 23:1-3).

> *"Justice, and only justice, you shall pursue, that you may live and possess the land which the Lord your God is giving you"* (Deuteronomy 16:20).

Justice must be based on what is true, not what is false. What is just is not determined by the wicked majority nor is it determined by our sympathies for the poor. Justice, determined by an objective standard of truth, must prevail. This is the only way for one's God-given rights to not be infringed upon.

X: Do Not Covet

"You shall not covet your neighbor's house; you shall not covet your neighbor's wife or his male servant or his female servant or his ox or his donkey or anything that belongs to your neighbor" (Exodus 20:17).

The first four commandments address our relationship with God. The next five deal with our actions as they relate to our fellow man. The last commandment is a little different. It is solely about what we think.

This shows us that God expects more from us than just outward service. He knows our thoughts (Hebrews 4:12) and expects us to think a certain way. The proverb writer noted, *"For as he thinks within himself, so he is"* (Proverbs 23:7), and, *"Watch over your heart with all diligence, for from it flow the springs of life"* (Proverbs 4:23). Our virtue and morality must not be superficial; otherwise, they can be cast aside whenever it becomes convenient or somehow advantageous to us to act wickedly and immorally. For a society to work properly, people must be truly be good people and not just act like it when it is easy to do so.

But there are other relevant principles to be found in the prohibition against covetousness. One is that we must desire good for our neighbor. Paul said, *"Rejoice with those who rejoice, and weep with those who weep"* (Romans 12:15). If our neighbor is prosperous, we should not begrudge him or be jealous of him; we ought to rejoice with him for the blessings he has received. The ungodly spirit of covetousness is seen when a man wishes for the prosperous to be torn down in some hope that his own situation will improve. We have already discussed the importance of working hard to provide for oneself instead of desiring the blessings of others. Covetousness desires that one be denied the fruits of his labor for someone else's selfish benefit. A society cannot function well for long if the prosperous and successful are constantly being torn down in order to help those who have not been prosperous or successful.

There is also the principle of contentment that is found in the command against covetousness. We have already seen that *stealing* from others demonstrates a lack of contentment for the blessings which one has received from God. Covetousness, though it is merely a thought process and not an action, is an indicator of the same lack of contentment. Paul wrote, *"If we have food and covering, with these we shall be content"* (1 Timothy 6:8). If people are content with even the most basic necessities, instead of wishing for hardship and loss to befall others who have been more successful, society as a whole will be much better off.

Conclusion

The foundation of a godly society does not begin with government but with individuals. That is why these Ten Commandments are directed toward *individuals*. If we hope to have any chance of fixing our broken society, it must be done by changing the hearts and minds of the people.

If people would learn the principles and precepts contained in the Ten Commandments and put them into practice, our society will immediately and dramatically improve.

1. If we have no other gods, we will not place anything, even those in positions of civil authority, between us and the Lord.
2. If we refuse to worship idols, it will be due to the fact that we have faith in something unseen (God).

3. If we refrain from taking God's name in vain, it is because we have learned to respect and reverence the Lord.

4. If we remember the principles of the Sabbath day, we will be hardworking and remember the fact that God is our Creator.

5. If we honor our father and mother, we will take seriously our responsibility to care for them rather than leaving that responsibility to others (such as the government).

6. If we understand the commandment against murder, we will respect the sanctity of human life, which would necessarily include opposition to abortion and euthanasia.

7. If we understand the commandment against adultery, we will value both sexual purity and the institution of marriage.

8. If we understand the commandment against stealing, we will respect personal property rights, learn contentment, and work hard to provide for ourselves.

9. If we understand the commandment against bearing false witness, we will value honesty, truth, and justice.

10. If we understand the commandment against covetousness, we will realize that our thoughts, as well as our actions, must be righteous and that we should desire good for others and not hardship or loss.

Just imagine how much better our society would be if people simply lived according to these principles. Many, though — both on the "left" and the "right" — see the problems that exist in society and believe that there must be some government action, program, or law that could correct them. But this is a poor substitute for a free people acting according to Biblical principles.

There is a role which God has ordained for civil government. But there is also a danger in expanding the power and responsibility of government beyond the divinely-ordained role.

5

WHAT GOD "ORDAINED" WITH RESPECT TO CIVIL GOVERNMENT

Bible students have long differed over the nature and role of civil government. The Bible tells us to *"be subject unto the higher powers"* (Romans 13:1, KJV) and to *"submit to every ordinance of man for the Lord's sake"* (1 Peter 2:13, KJV); but it also tells us that *"we must obey God rather than men"* (Acts 5:29). On the one hand, we are obligated to obey civil authorities; but on the other hand, civil authorities are not always right and cannot always be obeyed.

- Following the birth of Christ, Roman authorities killed all male babies two years old and younger in the region of Bethlehem (Matthew 2:16). In compliance with God's instructions, the parents of Jesus took Jesus to Egypt to prevent His death.
- The Jesus story reminds us of Pharaoh's actions against the male babies of the Hebrews. He first ordered the Hebrew midwives to kill all male babies upon the birthing stools (*a form of partial birth abortion*, Exodus 1:15). The midwives refused to obey Pharaoh's orders, and God rewarded them with their own families. Pharaoh then ordered that all Hebrew male babies be thrown into the river (Exodus 1:22). *"By faith"* (Hebrews 11:23), the

parents of Moses refused to comply with Pharaoh's orders. They hid their son and took actions to preserve his life.

- The Babylonian government of Daniel's time ordered the execution of any person who refused to worship Nebuchadnezzar's idol god. Shadrach, Meshach and Abednego refused to obey the king's orders and were miraculously delivered by God (Daniel 3).

- The Medo-Persian king, Darius, was convinced by Daniel's political enemies to sign a law that forbade prayer to any man or god except Darius. The penalty was execution. Daniel deliberately disobeyed the injunction but was miraculously delivered by God (Daniel 6).

- According to John, God cast down the civil government described as *"the great whore of Babylon"* for persecuting and executing saints (Revelation 17:6; 18:24; 6:9-11).

- With the help and support of the Jews and their officials, the Roman government tortured and crucified the very Son of God.

- There are dozens of other Bible examples of godless and inhumane civil governments and their nefarious practices. In the 2000 years since the completion of the Bible, hundreds of additional godless governments have slaughtered tens of millions of innocent people. Given this reality — and considering what is now happening in the United States and other countries — it is wise for us to consider what the Bible teaches about civil government.

Romans 13: What God "Ordained"

A proper understanding of Romans 13 is essential to a proper understanding of civil government. At the heart of this understanding is a proper understanding of what God has *"ordained"* with respect to civil government. Many Bible students fall prey to Calvinistic errors with regard to "providence" when they read Romans 13:1. This error causes them to falsely conclude that God "appoints" specific leaders, administrations, or regimes. They believe the ordination of such leaders to be a *personal and direct act of God.* This view is both false and dangerous. It leads people to conclude that one must not question or challenge civil officials regardless of their policies lest one *"be found fighting against God,"* to use the words of Gamaliel (Acts 5:39).

The context of Romans 13 shows that God ordains, not the *style* of government or the *personnel* of government, *but the* ***function*** *of government.* This is easily seen from the *context* of Romans 13:1. Paul explains both the purpose and function of civil government:

> *"Let every person be subject to the governing authorities. For there is no authority except from God, and those that exist have been instituted by God. Therefore whoever resists the authorities resists what God has appointed, and those who resist will incur judgment. For rulers are not a terror to good conduct, but to bad. Would you have no fear of the one who is in authority? Then do what is good, and you will receive his approval. For he is God's servant for your good. But if you do wrong, be afraid, for he does not bear the sword in vain. For he is the servant of God, an avenger who carries out God's wrath on the wrongdoer"* (Romans 13:1-4, ESV).

People see the word *"instituted"* or *"ordained"* and automatically think of *direct* divine appointment of civil rulers. Some reach this conclusion because of their false views of providence and predestination. Others simply fail to distinguish between the dispensations of the Old and New Testaments. They attempt to interpret Romans 13:1 in a way that harmonizes with God's governing methods during the Old Testament Jewish *theocracy.* Of course, the Old Covenant has been replaced with the New Covenant (Hebrews 8:7-13; 9:15-17; 10:15-20); and the Law of Moses has been replaced with the Law of Christ (Hebrews 7:12; Colossians 2:14). We are not under a theocratic system of governance today. As Jesus said, new wine cannot be stored in old wineskins.

Many people think instantly of Daniel 4:32 when they think of Romans 13:1 (*governing authorities are ordained of God*). Daniel told Nebuchadnezzar that he needed to learn the lesson that *"... the Most High rules the kingdom of men and gives it to whom he will"* (Daniel 4:32, KJV). The phrases may sound similar, but the context is quite different. Babylon sacked Jerusalem, destroyed the Temple, and carried the Israelites away into captivity because God had "summoned" Babylon as His "bird of prey" (Isaiah 46:11) to execute His vengeance upon apostate Judah. Again, the Jewish religion was *theocratic.* The Jewish people were God's chosen and peculiar *nation* (Exodus 19:5-6). God intervened *directly* and *miraculously* at different times in both their preservation and their punishment. Those who believe that God continues to work through nations as He did under the Jewish theocracy need to answer this question: which "nation" is now being directly and miraculously managed by God? Which "nation" is now God's *chosen* and *peculiar* nation? None can be cited because in this dispensation the *church* is God's *holy nation* and *peculiar people* (1 Peter 2:9, KJV). The church is a *spiritual,* not a *civic,* kingdom. It is *"not of this world"* (John 18:36). Paul's instructions in Romans 13:1-4 address *civic* matters, not spiritual ones.

Implications For Other Institutions

Civil government is not the only divine institution. God also instituted the *home* and the *church*. If being "ordained" of God necessarily implies direct divine appointment of particular individuals in government, as some argue from Romans 13:1, then the institution of the home would imply direct divine selection of *marriage partners*; and the institution of the church would imply direct divine selection of *church members* (the individual "election" of Calvinistic predestination). Interestingly, some who *reject* Calvinistic election with respect to salvation *accept* it with respect to the appointment of civil authorities!

In instituting "the home," God instituted the *function and purpose* of the home. In instituting the church, God instituted the *function and purpose* of the church. In instituting civil government, God instituted the *function and purpose* of civil government.

The God-Ordained Function Of Civil Government

If Romans 13:1 means direct (miraculous) divine installment of specific leaders or regimes, then God personally installed *Hirohito* as emperor of Japan, *Mao Tse Tung* as communist leader of China, *Joseph Stalin* as dictator of the Soviet Union, *Pol Pot* as communist leader of Cambodia, *Adolf Hitler* as fascist leader of Germany, and *Benito Mussolini* as fascist leader of Italy. One would also have to say that God raised these men up for them to do what they did, which was to capriciously kill one hundred million people. God did not "ordain" state sponsored persecution and slaughter of Christians, as was done by Rome (Acts 12:1-3; Revelation 17:6; 18:24). He does not "ordain" the indiscriminate slaughter of people based upon their ethnicity as done by Stalin, Hitler, Hussein, and Milosevic; nor does He ordain the current ethnic cleansing occurring in Mindanao, the Philippines, the Sudan, and elsewhere. God does not "ordain" the cruel and merciless slaughter of 1.5 million human babies every year in the United States and millions more each year in China and elsewhere. He does not "ordain" the passage of laws authorizing gay marriage and other godless behavior.

Some say that God directly appoints civil leaders but that He does not cause or approve their actions. This will not fit with their use of Daniel 4:32, for God *did* ordain the function of the Babylonians and the Assyrians as instruments of His wrath. Assyria was "dispatched" by God in order to subjugate Israel; similarly, Babylon was later "summoned" against Judah. Assyria served as a *"rod"* in God's hand against the northern kingdom of Israel (Isaiah 10:5-6). Those who believe the "ordaining" of Romans 13:1 to be defined by God's actions with respect to Nebuchadnezzar, Cyrus and Sennacherib must understand that God raised these men up because of what they would do as His punishing "servants" (Isaiah 46:11; 44:28; 45:1; 10:5). The *functions* of these men were as ordained as the men themselves.

So, what function does God have in mind for *today's* civil authorities? The New Testament answers this question. It sets forth the *divinely approved model* of civil government. The purpose of government — as stated by the apostles (Romans 13:3, 4; 1 Peter 2:14) — is to *punish evildoers and approve those who do what is right.* It is a government that is *"not a cause of fear for good behavior, but for evil."* It praises those who *"do what is good"* (Romans 13:3). Peter wrote, *"Submit yourselves to every ordinance of man for the Lord's sake: whether it be to the king as supreme; or unto governors, as unto them that are sent by him for the punishment of evildoers, and for the praise of them that do well"* (1 Peter 2:13-14, KJV).

God tells us to pray for civil authorities that we may lead *"a quiet and peaceable life in all godliness and honesty"* (1 Timothy 2:2, KJV). The word translated "quiet" is a word that emphasizes *tranquility arising from the absence of outward disturbance.* The word translated "peaceable" emphasizes a *tranquility arising from within.* While this is primarily a *prayer* passage, we learn from it an important function of civil rulers: they are to provide peaceful and secure conditions in which citizens are *free* to live lives according to divinely revealed principles of conduct and behavior.

The God-ordained model of government is one that:

- Provides for the safety and security of its citizens (1 Timothy 2:2).
- Provides an atmosphere in which its citizens may live peacefully, mind their own affairs, and work with their own hands, doing what is right for themselves, their families and their neighbors (1 Thessalonians 4:11; 1 Timothy 5:8; Romans 13:1-10).
- Punishes those whose actions are harmful and detrimental to the divinely ordained function of society.

Any government that fails or refuses to follow this model cannot be classified as a God-ordained government.

Conclusion

Paul concluded his comments about civil government by explaining how (civil) laws are fulfilled when people fulfill "the royal law" or "second great commandment," which is to *"love your neighbor as yourself"* (James 2:8; Matthew 22:39; Romans 13:8). He cited certain civil laws and explains how they are "briefly summarized" in the action of loving one's neighbor. *"Love does no harm to a neighbor; therefore, love is the fulfillment of the law"* (Romans 13:10, NKJV). Thus, the need for civil law is eliminated when citizens behave according to divine principles.

Solomon said, *"Righteousness exalts a nation, but sin is a reproach to any people"* (Proverbs 14:34, ESV). *"Righteousness"* involves one's treatment of his fellow man. When exercised by the members of any nation, the principles of righteousness will elevate that nation. Honesty, integrity, justice, fairness, generosity, personal responsibility, and respect for others are just a few of the qualities that are embodied in righteousness. History tells us that as long as the people of a nation abide by these principles, their nation is exalted.

Obviously, not all governments function according to the God-ordained model. When governments ignore or depart from their divinely specified function, they soon begin to infringe upon citizen's rights: hindering their freedoms, crushing their spirits, and stifling their productivity. As we have seen, some governments become so wicked that they slaughter their own people. According to history, governments have committed most of the violence that has been inflicted upon mankind.

Because of their knowledge of biblical principles of conduct, Bible students are those who are best qualified to speak and act in ways that best influence government and society. Let us not be afraid to say and do what is necessary to cultivate a God-ordained government.

6

A MINISTER OF GOD, OR OF SATAN?

Christians live in the world but are not of the world (Romans 12:2). We are part of a kingdom that is spiritual and eternal (John 18:36; Daniel 2:44). Yet while here on the earth, we live under the rule of civil authorities. How are we, as Christians, to view these leaders?

Paul told the Christians in Rome that they were to be subject to the civil authorities:

> "*Every person is to be in subjection to the governing authorities. For there is no authority except from God, and those which exist are established by God. Therefore whoever resists authority has opposed the ordinance of God; and they who have opposed will receive condemnation upon themselves*" (Romans 13:1-2).

However, Paul did not mean that we are to obey the civil authorities unconditionally. When ordered not to preach about Christ, Peter told the Sanhedrin council, "*We must obey God rather than men*" (Acts 5:29). Obedience to God is our first priority. We are to be subject to the civil authorities *only if* our subjection to them does not require the forsaking of our God-given instructions and responsibilities.

A Minister of God

When we study Paul's teaching about government in Romans 13, we must do so with the above disclaimer clearly in mind. Government is not the ultimate authority — God is. Further, He has given a specific role for the civil authorities.

> *"For rulers are not a cause of fear for good behavior, but for evil. Do you want to have no fear of authority? Do what is good and you will have praise from the same; for it is a minister of God to you for good. But if you do what is evil, be afraid; for it does not bear the sword for nothing; for it is a minister of God, an avenger who brings wrath on the one who practices evil"* (Romans 13:3-4).

Government is called a minister of God. A minister is a servant. What role does government serve in God's providential care for mankind? Government exists to punish those who do evil, to protect those who do good, and to allow its people the freedom to live and worship according to God's instructions (Romans 13:3-4; 1 Timothy 2:1-4). A government that fulfills this role is God's minister because it is doing the work He has given it to do.

But what if a government is not doing this? Instead of protecting the innocent, they allow the innocent to be victimized; or they themselves actively persecute Christians. Instead of punishing evildoers, they ignore or even reward their crimes. Instead of allowing us the freedom to serve God according to His will, they attempt to silence gospel preaching or prohibit Christians from assembling. Is such a government still *"a minister of God to you for good"* (Romans 13:4)?

Some will automatically affirm that an oppressive government is still God's minister. But is that conclusion demanded by the context in Romans 13? And does the rest of the New Testament support this?

A Minister of Satan

In the book of Revelation, the Lord warned the church in Smyrna of the persecution that was coming. He said, "*The devil is about to cast some of you into prison, so that you will be tested, and you will have tribulation for ten days*" (Revelation 2:10). This persecution was being carried out by the civil authorities (the Roman government). Were these authorities acting as the minister of God here when they persecuted Christians? On the contrary, they were doing the work of the devil. Their service to Satan is so plainly indicated here that their work of throwing Christians into prison is attributed to the devil himself.

When a government rejects its God-given role and begins to do harm to the ones who should be enjoying its protection, that government ceases to be a minister of God and becomes a minister of Satan.

Our Responsibility as Christians

The Scriptures teach that a government can act as either the minister of God or the minister of Satan. As Christians, what is our responsibility toward the government?

We are to pray for all leaders, whether they are doing their divinely-appointed work or not. Notice what Paul says:

> "*First of all, then, I urge that entreaties and prayers, petitions and thanksgivings, be made on behalf of all men, for kings and all who are in authority, so that we*

> *may lead a tranquil and quiet life in all godliness and*
> *dignity. This is good and acceptable in the sight of God*
> *our Savior, who desires all men to be saved and to come*
> *to the knowledge of the truth"* (1 Timothy 2:1-4).

A government allowing its people the freedom to live their lives according to God's instructions is the ideal condition for the spread of the gospel. If this condition currently exists, we must pray for our leaders that they would allow it to continue. If it does not exist, we must pray that our leaders might have a change of heart or else be replaced by those who will be more favorable to the free spread of the gospel.

For those governments that are fulfilling their role as God's ministers, we are to be subject to them. After stating the role of civil government and labeling it as God's minister, Paul said this:

> *"Therefore it is necessary to be in subjection, not only*
> *because of wrath, but also for conscience'*
> *sake"* (Romans 13:5).

Paul began that phrase with the word *therefore*. The reason for being in subjection is stated in the previous verses. We must be in subjection to the government *because* the government is acting as God's minister, fulfilling the role He has given for the civil authorities.

What if the government is acting as a minister of Satan? First, we must be prepared to do what the church at Smyrna was told to do — endure whatever persecution and tribulation might come (Revelation 2:10). Second, we must refuse to submit to any law that requires us to forsake a divinely-given command or responsibility (Acts 5:29). Third, we should follow this principle: *"If possible, so far as it depends on you, be at peace with all men"* (Romans 12:18). If we can continue to serve God without drawing undue attention to ourselves, we ought to do so. This does not mean compromising on matters that pertain to the faith, but it means keeping a low profile so the wicked leaders will leave us alone as much as possible.

Remember God

Whether we live under good leaders or evil leaders, we must remember the One who is over all. In addressing our responsibility to civil authorities, Peter said, *"Act as free men, and do not use your freedom as a covering for evil, but use it as bondslaves of God"* (1 Peter 2:16).

Even though we may be citizens of a country here, we are primarily citizens of the kingdom of heaven (Philippians 3:20). Therefore, whether the government's rule warrants our submission (Romans 13:1-5) or our rebellion (Acts 5:29), we must always remain servants of God.

Following His death, burial, resurrection, and ascension into heaven, Jesus was placed *"far above all rule and authority and power and dominion, and every name that is named, not only in this age but also in the one to come"* (Ephesians 1:21). Jesus is over all and we will all give an account of our lives before Him (2 Corinthians 5:10). Therefore, we must do all things *"in the name of the Lord Jesus"* (Colossians 3:17), regardless of what our rulers may say about it.

7

THE PERILS OF A STRONG, CENTRALIZED GOVERNMENT

Power and control are becoming centralized in Washington, D.C. One of the most notable examples of this is the Affordable Care Act which, at the time of this writing, has just been upheld by the Supreme Court. The word of God contains warnings of the dangers that are presented by a strong, centralized government. It also contains teachings that will help us deal with this. Currently in our country, an expanding government is a reality. Let us turn to God's word for wisdom and instruction in dealing with this present condition.

The Manner of a King

In the days of Samuel as he acted as judge over Israel, the people came to him and demanded, *"Give us a king to judge us"* (1 Samuel 8:5). This displeased Samuel, but it was not until after he received counsel from the Lord that he warned the people of the perils of having a king. It should not be surprising that such trouble would exist. After all, their demanding of a king amounted to a rejection of God and His rule (1 Samuel 8:7). Problems always arise when people follow a different path than the one God shows them. This is the warning Samuel delivered from God to the people:

> *"This will be the procedure of the king who will reign over you: he will take your sons and place them for himself in his chariots and among his horsemen and they will run before his chariots. He will appoint for himself commanders of thousands and of fifties, and some to do his plowing and to reap his harvest and to make his weapons of war and equipment for his chariots. He will also take your daughters for perfumers and cooks and bakers.*
>
> *"He will take the best of your fields and your vineyards and your olive groves and give them to his servants. He will take a tenth of your seed and of your vineyards and give to his officers and to his servants. He will also take your male servants and your female servants and your best young men and your donkeys and use them for his work. He will take a tenth of your flocks, and you yourselves will become his servants"* (1 Samuel 8:11-17).

The people were only thinking of the perceived benefits of having a king — *"our king may judge us and go out before us and fight our battles"* (1 Samuel 8:20). A king *could* do those things, but he would not necessarily do so. But what every king would do, regardless of whether he was a good or bad king, was *take* from the people — *take* their sons, *take* their daughters, *take* their servants, *take* their property, *take* their resources — with the result being that the people ultimately would be enslaved to the king. The reality was that he would be more than a judge and military leader; he would be their master and the people would be his servants.

After warning about this centralization of power and authority under someone other than God, Samuel told the people: *"Then you will cry out in that day because of your king whom you have chosen for yourselves, but the Lord will not answer you in that day"* (1 Samuel 8:18). Once this was done, it would be too late to change back to the state in which they were before. They would have to deal with a new reality.

As our government grows and becomes more powerful, we may reach a point in which we will not be able to go back to the life we knew before. We will have to deal with that new reality. As troubling as this thought may be, with the Bible as our guide, we can face whatever may be in our future.

The Divinely Ordained Role of Civil Government

The children of Israel were going to face hardship under a king because a king was a rejection of God's plan. God was to be their king. Instead, they wanted a human king so they could be *"like all the nations"* (1 Samuel 8:20). We live in a different time today. While human government was initially established by man as a rebellion against God (see chapter 3), He is able to use civil authorities for His purpose. Therefore, He has ordained civil government with certain roles:

- **Punish evildoers** — *"For rulers are not a cause of fear for good behavior, but for evil. [...] But if you do what is evil, be afraid; for it does not bear the sword for nothing; for it is a minister of God, an avenger who brings wrath on the one who practices evil"* (Romans 13:3-4). This is one of the fundamental roles that God has given to government — to punish those who do evil.
- **Protect the innocent** — Related to the punishment of evildoers, the government is also to protect citizens from being harmed by others. In outlining the role of punishing evil, Paul wrote that government is *"a minister of God to you for*

good" (Romans 13:4). They are to punish criminals and protect the rest of the population from such individuals.

- **Provide and maintain a free environment** — Paul told Timothy that prayers were to be made for those in authority "*so that we may lead a tranquil and quiet life in all godliness and dignity*" (1 Timothy 2:2). This is what God intends for governments to do. They are to allow people to have the freedom to serve God and carry out their daily responsibilities without being harassed or hindered by the authorities or any other group.

Man has many ideas for government beyond these roles. But no matter what government does, these roles should take precedence. Why? Because these are the divinely ordained roles for civil government. Israel rejected God's plan in demanding a king and would face negative consequences for it. In the same way, there will be negative consequences that will naturally follow when government neglects the role that God has given by focusing on other things. The further a government moves away from these roles, the more negative consequences there will be. Naturally, a national government will affect a far greater number of people than a local government.

What Should We Expect as the Government Becomes More Powerful?

Just as there were consequences for a strong centralized government in Samuel's day, there are consequences today. We must be prepared for them.

Expect less freedom — We have been greatly blessed to live in a free society in this country. Even with the changes that are taking place, we still have more liberty than many people around the world. But as the government grows in power, we will lose more of our freedom. This is just a reality that we must prepare for as the civil authorities assume more control over our lives. Some losses of freedom may seem inconsequential, while others that relate to our families or our service to God will be a much bigger deal.

Expect higher taxes — As the government grows, its need for revenue also increases. This money needs to come from somewhere. In our country, expect this increase in government revenue to come from higher taxes. As taxes increase, we will still have two responsibilities that will not change — we must continue to pay our taxes (Matthew 22:21; Romans 13:7), and we must still provide for our own (1 Timothy 5:8).

But how can we continue to provide for our own if our taxes keep going up? First, we must be prepared to work harder. Notice Paul's example to the brethren in Thessalonica: "*We kept working night and day so that we would not be a burden to any of you; not because we do not have the right to this, but in order to offer ourselves as a model for you, so that you would follow our example*" (2 Thessalonians 3:8-9). From Paul's example we learn that when times are hard, we work harder.

We also must be prepared to live with less. We may not enjoy the standard of living to which we have become accustomed. But we can manage. Paul said, "*I have learned to be content in whatever circumstances I am. I know how to get along with humble means, and I also know how to live in prosperity; in any and every circumstance I have learned the secret of being filled and going hungry, both of having abundance and suffering need. I can do all things through Him who strengthens me*" (Philippians 4:11-13). Contentment is going to be a very important attitude going into the future.

Expect inefficiency — The wise man who authored the book of Ecclesiastes wrote about what he learned as he observed and experienced life *"under the sun"* (Ecclesiastes 1:14).

One of the things he observed was the effect of government bureaucracy. Many in this country want bigger government. There are those currently in office who are pushing for this as well with increased spending, regulations, and powers. Notice what the wise man had to say about the benefits of bigger government:

> *"If you see the oppression of the poor and the denial of justice and righteousness in the province, do not be shocked at the sight; for one official watches over another official, and there are higher officials over them"* (Ecclesiastes 5:8).

Notice that he does not mention a benefit of bigger government. The poor were oppressed and justice and righteousness were denied *despite* (or perhaps *because of*) the bureaucracy.

Someone might ask how this can be. The officials in place are supposed to make sure the poor are helped and that justice is carried out. But this is the way it is. Look at our country. Despite all the money the government spends to help the poor and all the programs they have started, poverty is still a problem. So many people who are looking to the government to help remain in their poor condition. Some will say we need more programs or that we need to spend more money. The wise man observed and noted that this will not work. Make government bigger. Expand the bureaucracy. The poor will still be oppressed, and justice and righteousness will still be denied.

The problem is this: the more government grows and the more it tries to provide, the more people put their trust in and rely upon the government. This is completely contrary to what the Bible teaches. We are told, *"Trust in the Lord with all your heart"* (Proverbs 3:5), not trust in the civil government. We are to *"draw near with confidence to the throne of grace,"* not to the seat of government, *"so that we may... find grace to help in time of need"* (Hebrews 4:16).

According to the Bible, civil government has a certain role: provide and maintain a secure environment, punish evildoers, and protect the innocent (1 Timothy 2:2-3; Romans 13:3-4). A large bureaucracy is not needed to do these things. Big government does not make things better. Turning to God and doing things His way is what makes things better.

Expect idolatry — Luke records the event that led to God punishing Herod the king. *"On an appointed day Herod, having put on his royal apparel, took his seat on the rostrum and began delivering an address to them. The people kept crying out, 'The voice of a god and not of a man!'"* (Acts 12:21-22). Some people today, especially in this country, look to government or politicians as their god.

It is easy to draw a comparison between Herod and certain government leaders today. Herod was praised for his speech and likened to deity. Certain ones today use their polished and inspiring speeches and, as a result, are deified by men.

Many politicians have led people to put their trust and faith in the government. How have they done this? They have done this by providing more and more aid and services so that people learn to rely on the government. This is what Herod was said to have done prior to the record of the people praising him. Luke told us that *"their country was fed by the king's country"* (Acts 12:20).

God's plan for government is simple: keep the peace, punish evildoers, and beyond that, leave us alone (Romans 13:4; 1 Timothy 2:2). In our country, men have added education, health care, retirement, stabilization of the economy, and more to the work of the civil government. As a result, many people now immediately turn to the government to provide their basic needs and to be the source of help in difficult times. They rely on the government and have put their faith in politicians. God does not look kindly upon those who accept such praise, as we see in the example of Herod, who was *"eaten by worms and died"* (Acts 12:23).

Expect persecution — It should not surprise us that persecution will come from the government as it grows more powerful. Those who set themselves up as god will persecute believers of the one true God. Persecution is a reality for Christians anyway (2 Timothy 3:12; 1 Peter 4:12,16); and it is often worst when the source is government. Since the church was established in the first century, severe persecution is often the work of the civil authorities.

Do not be caught off guard by this. Instead, be ready for it; and do not be intimidated. The second time Peter and John were brought before the Council, they were told: *"We gave you strict orders not to continue teaching in this name, and yet, you have filled Jerusalem with your teaching and intend to bring this man's blood upon us."* Were they intimidated? Not at all. They simply answered, *"We must obey God rather than men"* (Acts 5:28-29). One day the government may try to stop you from serving God, assembling with fellow Christians, or teaching the gospel to others. When this happens, do not be afraid. Peter later wrote, *"But even if you should suffer for the sake of righteousness, you are blessed, 'And do not fear their intimidation, and do not be troubled'"* (1 Peter 3:14).

What Do We Need to Do?

Knowing what we can expect as government becomes more powerful, what are we to do? The Bible helps us answer this question as well.

Be subject to civil authorities — Paul told the Romans, *"Every person is to be in subjection to the governing authorities"* (Romans 13:1). Likewise, Peter wrote, *"Submit yourselves for the Lord's sake to every human institution"* (1 Peter 2:13). Peter went on to say that even though we submit to civil authorities, we are *"free men"* (1 Peter 2:16). But one of the reasons we submit is so that we do not cause a hindrance to the gospel. *"For such is the will of God that by doing right you may silence the ignorance of foolish men"* (1 Peter 2:15). As long as obedience to the government does not cause us to disobey God (Acts 5:29), we must be subject to those in authority.

Pray for those in power — Paul urged that prayers be made *"for kings and all who are in authority, so that we may lead a tranquil and quiet life in all godliness and dignity"* (1 Timothy 2:2). Notice that Paul does not say we are necessarily to pray for our leaders to have a long life or success in their political pursuits. In some cases, those may be fine. But what is more important is that they allow people the freedom to live a *"tranquil and quiet life."* Paul said, *"This is good and acceptable in the sight of God our Savior, who desires all men to be saved and to come to the knowledge of the truth"* (1 Timothy 2:3-4). A government that allows its people to be free makes the spread and practice of the gospel easier. Powerful, oppressive governments cause a hindrance to the preaching of God's saving word.

Take care of yourself — We need to do what we can to take care of ourselves, rather than being *"a burden to any"* (2 Thessalonians 3:8). If at all possible, we must provide for ourselves. Paul wrote, *"if anyone is not willing to work, then he is not to eat, either"* (2 Thessalonians 3:10). Notice that this is about *willingness*. If one is *unable* to care for himself, it should be expected that others step in to help. But if we are able to provide for ourselves, even if it means *"working night and day"* (2 Thessalonians 3:8), we need to do so. Paul explains the seriousness of this responsibility to Timothy: *"if anyone does not provide for his own, and especially for those of his household, he has denied the faith and is worse than an unbeliever"* (1 Timothy 5:8).

Be willing to help others — We also need to be willing to help those in need. Again, this will take extra work on our part. *"He who steals must steal no longer; but rather he must labor, performing with his own hands what is good, so that he will have something to share with one who has need"* (Ephesians 4:28). Do not think that you are relieved of your responsibility to help the needy simply because the government attempts to do so. There will still be people in need, even with the government expanding its powers to deal with the problem. It should not surprise us that a big government fails to do what it promises. The wise man noted, *"If you see oppression of the poor and denial of justice and righteousness in the province, do not be shocked at the sight; for one official watches over another official, and there are higher officials over them"* (Ecclesiastes 5:8). The huge bureaucracy put in place to solve these problems will be too inefficient to do so. While the government is busy helping those who do not need or deserve help, we need to do what we can to help those who are truly in need.

Conclusion

As the federal government in our country becomes more and more powerful, we must face the new challenges in the way that God expects from His servants. But we should also remember that no matter how strong a government might be, eventually it will fall (Proverbs 27:24). There is only one kingdom that endures forever (Daniel 2:44). That is God's kingdom.

In the Sermon on the Mount, Jesus said, "*Seek first His kingdom and His righteousness*" (Matthew 6:33). Remember that "*our citizenship is in heaven, from which also we eagerly wait for a Savior, the Lord Jesus Christ*" (Philippians 3:20). No matter what happens in this country, we "*desire a better country*" (Hebrews 11:16).

As Christians, our king is Jesus Christ. No human ruler will ever surpass Him in providing mercy, justice, benevolence, or hope. Nor is there anyone more deserving of our trust and allegiance than He is. Remember the role of government. Remember your role to government. Most importantly, remember your need to serve Him who is "*far above all rule and authority and power and dominion, and every name that is named, not only in this age but also in the one to come*" (Ephesians 1:21).

8

LIMITATIONS OF CIVIL GOVERNMENT

Whether we accept the divinely-appointed role for civil government or believe that rulers ought to have some other mission, we need to understand the fact that a human governing body has certain limitations. These limitations are inherent and will always be true, regardless of time, place, or political party.

These limitations which we will consider in this chapter should remind us of two things. First, we ought not put our trust in *any* human government. Second, we should be wary of granting too much authority to those who rule over us.

Civil Governments are Made Up of Imperfect Humans

The most fundamental limitation of any human government is simply the fact that it is made up of mere men. No one has lived a life of sinless perfection like Jesus did (1 Peter 2:22). Instead, *"all have sinned and fall short of the glory of God"* (Romans 3:23). Logically, we know this. We know that everyone is fallible. Yet many ignore how this truth about *humans* is translated into the workings of *human* governments. The fallibility of man is often compounded when government is involved.

Suppose you had a government that strictly limited itself to the role for which God ordained it. Of course, no human government has so limited itself. But assume for a moment that such a government existed that determined to do nothing more than punish evildoers, protect the innocent, and provide and maintain a free environment for its people. Could we put our trust in such a government? Of course not. Those leaders, despite the noble goal of limiting themselves to their divinely-given role, would rule imperfectly. Evildoers would occasionally escape punishment either because the authorities would be unable to locate and capture them, or because they would have a limited knowledge of events that transpired, preventing them from proving their case against the evildoer or from even being aware of the criminal activity. It would also sometimes happen that they would punish alleged evildoers but would be incorrect in their judgment and would be punishing the innocent instead. These things occasionally happen now. Strictly limiting the government to the specific tasks which God ordained for it would not result in the elimination of mistakes and failures to punish evildoers, protect the innocent, and provide freedom for its citizens.

The above scenario of a government attempting to carry out completely their divinely-given role and nothing more is purely hypothetical. The reality is that all civil governments (each to a varying degree) have taken much more authority over their citizens than God has granted them. The fact that these governments are made up of fallible human beings should cause all of us to be very hesitant to call for more and more power to be ceded over to these human rulers.

If you assume the best of them — that they want to do good for others and help those in need, not for political reasons, but out of the goodness of their hearts — you are still left with imperfect humans trying to do perform these good works. Of course, these people could also be corrupt and evil — only concerned with power, glorifying themselves, and even harming those they dislike for whatever reason — because they are, after all, fallible human beings.

Fallible people with good intentions and bad intentions exist outside of government as well. But there is a greater danger when they are within government. Why? They have power *over* others. They can use the force of law and the threat of punishment to enforce their laws and enact their plans. The common man does not have this. When a regular citizen acts corruptly and wickedly, others may surely be negatively impacted, but not nearly to the degree as when the civil ruler acts corruptly and wickedly. And the greater the power that the ruler has, the greater the oppression of the citizens.

Civil Governments Cannot Take Care of Us

Too many people in our society want someone else to take care of them. A failure has taken place in their upbringing — whether through the fault of poor parenting, the influence of evil companions, the decline of society as a whole, or a combination of factors — such that they believe a certain standard of living is guaranteed to them, simply by virtue of the fact that they were born in a prosperous country. So whether they need food, shelter, clothing, health care, or anything that is (or is thought to be) a basic necessity, they become accustomed to looking to the government to provide whatever they cannot (or will not) provide for themselves.

Unfortunately, civil government is simply incapable of taking care of its citizens — at least not adequately over a prolonged period of time. The abject poverty and collapse of socialist and communist countries serve as examples to prove this point. But why can governments not adequately take care of their citizens? Besides the fact that they are made up of fallible human beings who, even with the best of intentions, will never be able to do all that they want to do to help others, there is a fundamental flaw in the systems they set up.

> "*If you see oppression of the poor and denial of justice and righteousness in the province, do not be shocked at the sight; for one official watches over another official, and there are higher officials over them*" (Ecclesiastes 5:8).

This commentary on the ineffectiveness of a large government bureaucracy was the observation of Solomon, the head of the civil government in Israel. He noted that it should not be shocking when oppression and injustice exist, despite the presence of bureaucracies that, theoretically, ought to prevent or help alleviate such conditions. Yet Solomon saw that an extensive network and hierarchy of government officials overseeing the people are incapable of doing what they are supposed to do (even if the leaders and/or the bureaucrats have good intentions). The larger the bureaucracy, the more unaccountable and inefficient it becomes. This principle is universally true. Yet many Bible believers ignore Solomon's words (or are oblivious to them) and call upon government to do more and more to take care of us.

God never intended for civil government to take care of us. He has a different plan for this. It begins with His providence. In creating this world, God *provided* everything we need in order to survive: plants and animals for food (Genesis 1:29; 9:3), proper conditions for survival (Acts 14:17), and the ability to work in order to provide for ourselves (Acts 17:28; 2 Thessalonians 3:10).

If one is unable to provide for himself, God has made provisions for such a one to be cared for — and not by the civil government. Individuals can help (Galatians 6:9-10). One's family can help (1 Timothy 5:4, 16). In certain cases, the church can help (Acts 4:32-35). If everyone tried to help others according to their *ability* and *opportunity* (2 Corinthians 8:12; Galatians 6:10) rather than thinking that a government "safety net" absolves us of our responsibility to do good to others, the number of people who would yet require government assistance would be drastically reduced.

The Scriptures teach that we can survive *without* government through the providence of God. The wise man explained this:

> *"Know well the condition of your flocks, and pay attention to your herds; for riches are not forever, nor does a crown endure to all generations. When the grass disappears, the new growth is seen, and the herbs of the mountains are gathered in, the lambs will be for your clothing, and the goats will bring the price of a field, and there will be goats' milk enough for your food, for the food of your household, and sustenance for your maidens"* (Proverbs 27:23-27).

Knowing that governments will, from time to time, collapse, Solomon explains how we can survive under such circumstances. By using what God has provided in His creation, we can have food, clothing, and the ability to participate in free market commerce. With "firm reliance on...divine Providence," we can survive without an oppressive, burdensome, and inefficient government machine trying (allegedly) to take care of us.

Civil Governments Cannot Legislate Morality

Religious people often want the government to enact certain legislation that would criminalize various forms of immorality. Their intentions may be good. After all, we know *"Righteousness exalts a nation, but sin is a disgrace to any people"* (Proverbs 14:34). Therefore, they support or advocate laws that criminalize gambling, prostitution, the use of drugs and alcohol, and so on. Unfortunately, civil governments are wholly incapable of keeping citizens from such vices.

Before we proceed any further, let me be *absolutely clear* that the practices I mentioned are wrong. But the point I wish to show is that civil government cannot adequately deal with these sins.

Of course, there are some immoral practices that the government *must* punish, such as murder, rape, theft, etc. The divinely-given role of civil government is to *"bear the sword"* in order to bring *"wrath on the one who practices evil"* (Romans 13:4). But how can we know what immorality the government should punish and what it should not?

God's plan for civil government and the reason why it is to *"bear the sword"* is to provide and maintain an environment in which its citizens can *"lead a tranquil and quiet life in all godliness and dignity"* (1 Timothy 2:2). In other words, God ordained civil government for the purpose of punishing those who would bring harm to other people without their consent. Therefore, sins like murder, rape, and theft would fall within the sphere of government's role to prosecute.

However, sins like drug abuse and prostitution do not fall into the same category. While harm surely comes to those who abuse drugs and visit prostitutes, they engage in these sinful acts out of their own freewill. Though they are surely abusing their blessings, they are simply using their natural rights to do so, and as a result, *"receiving in their own persons the due penalty of their error"* (Romans 1:27).

The above examples may be extreme (drug abuse and prostitution), but I used them for that reason. No one in their right mind will argue that prostitution is moral or that using heroin or some other such drug is a righteous activity. So it is perfectly understandable for moral and religious people to desire laws that would attempt to curtail these activities.

However, we need to be mindful of the fact that a government that is eroding personal liberty in the name of outlawing personal immorality is potentially dangerous for godly people. How is that? It is certainly true that laws against certain drugs may not affect us. But what if the government decides that sugar, meat, milk, or other *"foods which God has created to be gratefully shared in by those who believe and know the truth"* (1 Timothy 4:3) are harmful to our bodies and must therefore be restricted or prohibited? (This is not hypothetical; there are places where such things have already been restricted, prohibited, or such has been proposed.) Would we then defend such legislation of "morality"?

Prostitution is certainly immoral behavior and most God-fearing people are content for it to be illegal. But what happens when the government decides to criminalize other actions it believes to be immoral? There are people who believe that disciplining children, teaching against sin, carrying out church discipline, and other divinely-mandated actions are *immoral*. If the government is given the authority to legislate morality, then those with such beliefs, if they have power or influence within government, can cause trouble for Christians. This goes directly against the Christian's prayer regarding civil authorities — *"that we may lead a tranquil and quiet life in all godliness and dignity"* (1 Timothy 2:2). A government with the power to *legislate* morality is a government with the power to *define* morality. This is more power than God gives civil government.

Furthermore, civil laws against immorality always fail. Prostitution is illegal, but we still have prostitutes. Various drugs are illegal, but we still have chronic drug abuse. Passing a law to criminalize these wicked acts does not change the hearts of those who are wicked. They will simply ignore the law or find some other way to satisfy their corrupt minds.

On the other end of the spectrum, knowing that civil government is incapable of legislating morality, some believe that government should rather *promote* immorality. An example of this is same-sex marriage. Many will argue that people are free to engage in homosexuality. This is true. The Bible teaches that each one of us has *free will* and can *choose* what we will do. But, having the ability to choose an activity does not make that activity right. Homosexuality is still a sin, even though one may choose to practice it (1 Timothy 1:10). Those who engage in the behavior receive *"in their own persons the due penalty of their error"* (Romans 1:27) and, if they do not repent, stand to lose their souls (1 Corinthians 6:9).

If people are free to (wrongfully) engage in homosexuality, does this mean that the government should *change* marriage to include same-sex couples? Some who are staunch advocates of personal liberty argue that this is the necessary conclusion. However, it is quite different when a government refrains from outlawing a practice than when it makes a law that *supports, condones, or establishes a practice.*

Homosexuality is wrong. But if civil authorities attempted to enact a law that would *outlaw* homosexuality, they would fail to eliminate the practice, just as they have failed to eliminate prostitution. However, passing legislation that would allow (or establish) same-sex marriage would be *supporting* and *condoning* the practice. Furthermore, by changing the definition of marriage, civil authorities would be going beyond their divinely-ordained role and usurping the authority of God. He created the institution of marriage (Mark 10:6-9). Therefore, He makes the definition of marriage.

Civil authorities cannot legislate morality because they are simply not designed to deal with personal immorality. We can hope, pray, and insist that they not support, condone, or establish immoral practices. But if they can outlaw and punish what they believe to be immoral — while we might not mind as long as their definition of morality opposes those practices we would condemn (such as prostitution) — we may find ourselves in a dangerous condition if (or rather, when) their definition of morality changes.

Civil Governments Cannot Advance the Cause of Christ

Preaching the gospel is a critically important work. Because of this, some Christians want to use any means and method they can think of to spread the gospel. Though not as common in our society, history shows us examples of men who have attempted to use the force of government to spread Christianity.

In the New Testament, we see that spreading the gospel is first an individual responsibility. When persecution arose in Jerusalem, the disciples *"who had been scattered went about preaching the word"* (Acts 8:4). All Christians must work to be able to *"make a defense"* of their beliefs before others (1 Peter 3:15). Beyond this, there is only one institution ordained by God to do the work of preaching — the local church (1 Timothy 3:15).

Government cannot spread the gospel, at least not the pure, unadulterated gospel. First of all, God has given government a different role (this was discussed in greater detail in chapter five). Second, civil government is simply not designed to spread the gospel. Civil government rules on the basis of human laws and enforces those laws with physical force. In the realm of spiritual matters, we must rely wholly on God's laws, not man's (1 Peter 4:11; Colossians 3:17). Furthermore, Jesus made it clear that physical force was not to be used to defend Him or to advance His cause. (Matthew 26:51-54; cf. 2 Corinthians 10:3-4).

Besides this, *if* we were to use government to advance the gospel, we must wrestle with this question: what gospel? This question is similar to the question about legislating morality. What standard will the government use? In this case, what gospel will they promote? Paul told us there were *different gospels* (Galatians 1:6-9). Those who follow these different gospels have deserted Christ. Those who advance these different gospels are to be *accursed*. If civil government were to try to advance the gospel, we would have no guarantee that they would be advancing the *true* gospel. During the time of the Crusades, the force of civil authority was used to advance (so-called) Christianity. But was it the pure, ancient gospel of Christ being promoted or a distortion of it? It was a distortion of the gospel. This is what will invariably happen when civil government is given the task of advancing the gospel.

Since government cannot be used to advance the gospel, the best we can hope for is *liberty*: the freedom to teach, assemble, worship, and live as God has instructed us; the absence of barriers that might be placed in the way of our attempts to serve the Lord; the freedom of speech, religion, assembly, and so on.

This is why Paul said we are to pray for our leaders — that we might be free to serve God unhindered by those in power (1 Timothy 2:1-2). Civil government is very limited in what it can do to help us serve the Lord. The best it can do is leave us alone.

9

OUR RESPONSIBILITY TO CIVIL AUTHORITIES

It is important for us as Christians to understand the responsibilities which God has given us toward the powers that be. To a certain extent we are to mind our own business (1 Thessalonians 4:11) and recognize that through God's providence, we can survive *without* government (as was discussed briefly in the previous chapter). Yet since civil government is a reality and God has ordained it for a specific purpose, we are to act a certain way toward it. How are we to act toward civil authorities? Peter described the underlying principle regarding our responsibility to civil authorities in this way:

> *"Act as free men, and do not use your freedom as a covering for evil, but use it as bondslaves of God"* (1 Peter 2:16).

Some may be surprised that I did not quote one of the passages that addresses our responsibility to *submit* to those in authority. That is certainly a responsibility, but the principle stated above is the foundation for that and all other responsibilities that Christians have toward human rulers. First and foremost, Christians are *"bondslaves of God."* This means that we *always* put God first, even over those in positions of civil authority.

Those in government are (or rather, ought to be) ministers of God (Romans 13:4), fulfilling the role which He has ordained for them. When civil authorities forget that God is the Lord and that we are *all* His servants, they strive to become lords over the people and place themselves *between* God and man. When this happens, it causes trouble for all of us. The wise man said, *"When the righteous increase, the people rejoice, but when a wicked man rules, people groan"* (Proverbs 29:2).

As we consider our responsibilities toward civil authorities, remember that we are to *"act as free men."* This, of course, does not mean that we do whatever we might desire without any consideration of rules or consequences. We are to act as free men within a standard of law. What law? Since we are to be *"bondslaves of God,"* the highest standard of law which we are to follow is God's law.

Therefore, the extent to which we follow civil authorities and civil laws is *limited* to whatever degree God *allows* us to follow them. So each of the responsibilities we have toward those in power — submitting to them, praying for them, honoring them, and paying taxes — has a *limit* or peculiar *focus* that has been given by God.

Submit to Them

As civil authorities have been given a certain role by God, so, too, have we been given a responsibility toward those in power. Paul told the Romans, *"Every person is to be in subjection to the governing authorities"* (Romans 13:1). Peter wrote, *"Submit yourselves for the Lord's sake to every human institution, whether to a king as the one in authority, or to governors as sent by him for the punishment of evildoers and the praise of those who do right. ...honor the king"* (1 Peter 2:13-17). We cannot ignore our civil leaders. We must submit to them.

However, our submission has limits — we cannot act contrary to the will of God. When the apostles were commanded to do something that would have violated a divine command (refrain from teaching about Christ), they replied, "*We must obey God rather than men*" (Acts 5:29). This is why it is so important that we pray for our leaders. If we follow the will of God and they reject the role God has given them, we will have trouble. This will not only affect us; but as we will notice in the next section, it will have a negative impact upon those who need to hear the gospel.

Pray for Them

One of our specific obligations in prayer is to pray for those in positions of civil authority. Paul made this clear in his first letter to the young evangelist Timothy:

> "*First of all, then, I urge that entreaties and prayers, petitions and thanksgivings, be made on behalf of all men, for kings and all who are in authority, so that we may lead a tranquil and quiet life in all godliness and dignity. This is good and acceptable in the sight of God our Savior, who desires all men to be saved and to come to the knowledge of the truth*" (1 Timothy 2:1-4).

Not only did Paul teach that Christians are to pray for their leaders, he told us *why* we are to pray for them. There is a specific desire for which we should pray that is according to the will of God. Before we consider this, let us be reminded again of the purpose for which God ordained civil authorities.

Although human governments involve themselves in many areas of life, the role for which God ordained them is rather limited. Paul wrote, "*For rulers are not a cause of fear for good behavior, but for evil. Do you want to have no fear of authority? Do what is good and you will have praise from the same; for it is a minister of God to you for good. But if you do what is evil, be afraid; for it does not bear the sword for nothing; for it is a minister of God, an avenger who brings wrath on the one who practices evil"* (Romans 13:3-4). God uses civil authority to act as His minister in punishing evildoers. By implication, this means that civil authorities are also to protect the innocent. Paul's instructions to Timothy also indicate that God desires the civil authorities to provide and maintain an environment in which we can *"lead a tranquil and quiet life in all godliness and dignity"* (1 Timothy 2:2).

In praying for our leaders, for what types of things should we pray? First, let us notice some things that are not *necessarily* among the things we must include in our prayers:

- **We are not *necessarily* to pray for a certain *form* of government (democracy, republic, monarchy, etc.).** Our country places a high value on democracy. While this can be good, a democracy only works when the country is made up of moral people. Otherwise, the majority can decide to persecute, rob, and even kill any minority group they wish. God ordained a *role* for government, not a *form* of government.
- **We are not *necessarily* to pray for the health and safety of the leaders.** Often this is good as it avoids instability within the government. But there are times when a leader's death means safety for God's people. Joseph had to flee to Egypt with Mary and Jesus because of the infanticide being carried out by Herod (Matthew 2:13-16). After Herod was dead, an angel informed Joseph that it was now safe to return to Israel (Matthew 2:19-21).
- **We are not *necessarily* to pray for the leaders' success.** If they are seeking to carry out the role

which God has ordained, good. But often their ambitions are contrary to their divinely given role.

The scope of our prayers for our leaders is narrowly defined by Paul. He said we must pray for them *"so that we may lead a tranquil and quiet life in all godliness and dignity"* (1 Timothy 2:2). This is accomplished by the authorities fulfilling their divinely given role. Paul said, *"This is good and acceptable in the sight of God our Savior"* (1 Timothy 2:3). Therefore, this is the *first priority* for which we should pray regarding those in government.

What Is a Tranquil and Quiet Life? There may be many things that we might associate with a tranquil and quiet life. But there are certain things from a Biblical standpoint that we should consider. There is one thing that each of these has in common — *freedom*.

- **Freedom to work and provide for ourselves** — Paul instructed the brethren in Thessalonica, *"Make it your ambition to lead a quiet life and attend to your own business and work with your hands, just as we commanded you, so that you will behave properly toward outsiders and not be in any need"* (1 Thessalonians 4:11-12). Some want to be free from working and having to provide for themselves. But Paul says working is included in the *"quiet life"* a Christian should live. To the degree which we are able, it is important that we provide for our own (1 Timothy 5:8) and not be dependent upon others (2 Thessalonians 3:7-10).
- **Freedom to assemble with our brethren and worship** — Both of these activities are vital for Christians. The Hebrew writer told us, *"Let us consider how to stimulate one another to love and good deeds, not forsaking our own assembling together, as is the habit of some, but encouraging one another; and all the*

more as you see the day drawing near" (Hebrews 10:24-25). Regarding worship, Jesus said, "*God is spirit, and those who worship Him must worship in spirit and truth*" (John 4:24). Assembling and worshipping are not optional.

- **Freedom to teach the gospel to others** — Jesus told His apostles in the Great Commission, "*Go therefore and make disciples of all the nations, baptizing them in the name of the Father and the Son and the Holy Spirit, teaching them to observe all that I commanded you*" (Matthew 28:19-20). Though not every aspect of the Commission applies to us today, we still have the responsibility to teach the gospel (1 Peter 3:15; Philippians 2:16; 1 Timothy 3:15).

- **Freedom from persecution** — Persecution can come either from the government as they act as a minister of Satan rather than of God (cf. Revelation 2:10) or from some other individual or group that ought to be punished by a properly functioning government (Romans 13:4). Persecution seeks to destroy the church as Saul nearly did in Jerusalem, driving the disciples out of the city (Acts 8:1). But the absence of persecution helps the church to grow. Notice what happened after Saul was converted and the persecution subsided: "*So the church throughout all Judea and Galilee and Samaria enjoyed peace, being built up; and going on in the fear of the Lord and in the comfort of the Holy Spirit, it continued to increase*" (Acts 9:31).

If these freedoms do not exist, our responsibilities before God remain unchanged. But it is preferable in God's sight — and certainly in ours, as well — to have these freedoms than to not have them. When we are free to do these things, then "*we may lead a tranquil and quiet life*" (1 Timothy 2:2).

Why Is This Important? Paul said it was *"good and acceptable in the sight of God"* that we are permitted to *"lead a tranquil and quiet life"* (1 Timothy 2:2-3). But why does God see this as good and acceptable? The answer is in the next verse: *"Who desires all men to be saved and to come to the knowledge of the truth"* (1 Timothy 2:4). The implication here is that a government that does not meet its divinely given role is a threat and an obstacle to the spread of the gospel.

The purpose of praying for a tranquil and quiet life is not for our own comfort or prosperity. Those are certainly benefits, but the primary purpose is something far more important than those.

The purpose of a tranquil and quiet life is so that the gospel can be taught freely and openly so that others can hear it. Once they hear it and believe it, they can obey it without interference. Those who have obeyed it can continue to follow the Lord and lead others to Him. These things can happen amidst persecution, but they happen far more effectively without persecution.

So we must pray *"for kings and all who are in authority, so that we may lead a tranquil and quiet life in all godliness and dignity. This is good and acceptable in the sight of God our Savior, who desires all men to be saved and to come to the knowledge of the truth"* (1 Timothy 2:2-4).

Honor Them

Another one of the responsibilities we have toward those in civil authority is to *honor* them.

> *"Honor all people, love the brotherhood, fear God, honor the king"* (1 Peter 2:17).

The command to *honor* emphasizes two things: *reverence* (respect) and placing an appropriate *value* on that which is being honored.

First of all, we are certainly to revere or respect those in positions of authority. The wise man said, "*My son, **fear the Lord and the king**; do not associate with those who are given to change*" (Proverbs 24:21). In concluding his remarks about the role of civil government, Paul wrote, "*Render to all what is due them: tax to whom tax is due; custom to whom custom; **fear to whom fear; honor to whom honor**"* (Romans 13:7).

However, there is a limit to the *fear* or *honor* we render to our civil leaders. We are certainly not to honor them to the same degree which we would honor God. This is what the people did with Herod, and we can clearly see what God thought of it.

> "*On an appointed day Herod, having put on his royal apparel, took his seat on the rostrum and began delivering an address to them. The people kept crying out, '**The voice of a god and not of a man!**' And immediately an angel of the Lord struck him because he did not give God the glory, and he was eaten by worms and died*" (Acts 12:21-23).

No human ruler is worthy of such worship. So the degree to which we honor and fear our rulers is limited by this.

Furthermore, the commandment to honor our leaders does not prohibit us from identifying and calling attention to their shortcomings and errors. Jesus called Herod "*that fox*" (Luke 13:32) which was certainly not a complement or a title of honor. When Paul and Silas were unlawfully beaten and imprisoned in Philippi, the leaders of the city had them released and requested that they leave quietly, undoubtedly so as not to draw attention to their error. But notice Paul's response:

"They have beaten us in public without trial, men who are Romans, and have thrown us into prison; and now are they sending us away secretly? No indeed! But let them come themselves and bring us out" (Acts 16:37).

The rulers were unaware to this point that Paul and Silas were Roman citizens (Acts 16:38). So while this was not a deliberate denial of the rights of citizenship, it was a case of severe neglegence in not finding out their citizenship status before punishing them. This presented a problem for the leaders in Philippi. They wanted the problem to go away, so they tried to get Paul and Silas to leave quickly and quietly. The responsibility to *honor* these men did not mean that Paul was required to help them escape accountability for their failures. They were wrong and took their stand against the preaching of the gospel. Therefore, it was perfectly legitimate for Paul, as a Christian, to draw attention to their deeds so that they might be exposed.

Second, we are to recognize the *value* of our rulers. What are our civil authorities worth? Some people value certain political figures based upon how much wealth they can confiscate from others and redistribute to them. No God-fearing person should use this as a standard for favorable judgment, for it demonstrates a spirit of covetousness and animosity toward others, simply based upon what they possess.

So how should we value our civil leaders? First of all, we can judge their worth based upon their *wisdom*. Notice the words of Solomon:

"A poor yet wise lad is better than an old and foolish king who no longer knows how to receive instruction" (Ecclesiastes 4:13).

"Wisdom strengthens a wise man more than ten rulers who are in a city" (Ecclesiastes 7:19).

Again, when we consider the honor we are to give civil authorities in regard to what they are worth, Solomon explains that *wisdom* is more beneficial than just anyone who happens to be in a position of authority.

We can also judge our leaders' worth by their defense of our rights. Consider the instructions given to King Lemuel:

> "*Open your mouth for the mute, for the rights of all the unfortunate. Open your mouth, judge righteously, and defend the rights of the afflicted and needy*" (Proverbs 31:8-9).

When this referred to the *rights* of the afflicted and needy, this was not some "right" to the fruits of another man's labor. Rather, it was a defense of one's God-given rights which include the freedom to move about and associate with those who might be able to help them to improve their lives. It is neither *just* nor *fair* for the government to target one group (in this case, the rich), attack one of their God-given rights (to own property and do with it what they please), in order to give the fruits of their labor to another group (the poor). "*You shall not follow the masses in doing evil... nor shall you be partial to a poor man in his dispute*" (Exodus 23:2-3). Justice is based upon truth, not personal circumstances.

Finally, the value of our leaders can be summarized in this: how closely do they conform to the role which God has given to them?

> "*For rulers are not a cause of fear for good behavior, but for evil. ...for it is a minister of God to you for good. But if you do what is evil, be afraid; for it does not bear the sword for nothing; for it is a minister of God, an avenger who brings wrath on the one who practices evil*" (Romans 13:3-4).

Immediately after identifying government's God-given role of punishing evildoers and protecting the innocent from harm, Paul said we are to render *honor* to whom honor is *due* (Romans 13:7). The implication is *not* that all civil leaders are worthy of honor and respect and that they are helpful as "*a minister of God to you for good*" (Romans 13:4). Instead, Paul's statement indicates that the *value* of a particular government and the degree to which we are obligated to *honor* them is directly related to their fulfillment of the purpose for which God ordained them.

Pay Taxes

The responsibility to pay taxes is one that often immediately comes to mind when Christians think of our responsibilities toward those in authority. The passage most often cited is the one in which the Pharisees and Herodians challenged Jesus to give an answer about paying taxes, hoping they could trap Him in His words.

> "'*Teacher, we know that You are truthful and teach the way of God in truth, and defer to no one; for You are not partial to any. Tell us then, what do You think? **Is it lawful to give a poll-tax to Caesar, or not?**' But Jesus perceived their malice, and said, 'Why are you testing Me, you hypocrites? Show Me the coin used for the poll-tax.' And they brought Him a denarius. And He said to them, 'Whose likeness and inscription is this?' They said to Him, 'Caesar's.' Then He said to them, '**Then render to Caesar the things that are Caesar's**; and to God the things that are God's*'"* (Matthew 22:16-21).

The next chapter contains a more in depth examination of taxation. But we should briefly notice here that our obligation to pay taxes, just like every other obligation we have toward civil government, is *limited*.

When Jesus said, *"Render to Caesar the things that are Caesar's"* (Matthew 16:21), He was not teaching that every possible level of taxation is legitimate. How do we know? It is founded in the principle contained in Peter's statement: *"We must obey God rather than men"* (Acts 5:29).

For the sake of argument, suppose that the government imposed a 100% tax on income, property, etc., meaning that *everything* you own and *everything* you gain is claimed by the government. Does God expect us to comply with this, or does this fall into the category of obeying God rather than men? Our primary obligation to obey God would prohibit compliance *if* God has given instructions regarding our resources. Has He? Of course He has! We are to provide for ourselves (2 Thessalonians 3:10), provide for our families (1 Timothy 5:8), contribute to the weekly collection of the church (1 Corinthians 16:1-2), and use some of what we have beyond this to help those who are in need (Ephesians 4:28; Galatians 6:10). Therefore, a level of taxation that hinders us from fulfilling our God-given responsibilities is excessive and immoral. As Christians, when it comes to the use of our money, property, and resources, we must choose to obey God rather than men.

10

THE BIBLE AND TAXATION

The recent Supreme Court ruling on the "Affordable Care Act" impresses upon us just how vulnerable we are to government tax mandates. The new health bill will cost Americans a great deal in *taxes, fees,* and *regulations.* Those who have studied the law say that it contains 21 new taxes and constitutes the largest tax increase in American history. Unless this law is repealed, our taxes will go up, certain freedoms will be lost, and the job recovery will be hindered.

Paying taxes is both a civic and moral duty. However, there is no logical, legal, or moral reason why taxes should be punitive, burdensome, and oppressive. We shall see, both from biblical and secular history, that exorbitant taxation stifles economic growth and turns citizens into slaves. We will learn that God never intended for people to be burdened by excessive taxation and that people come under heavy tax burdens, not because of God, but because of their over reliance upon government. We will learn that God "ordained" the *function* of government and that a God-ordained government is quite limited in its scope and size. Since tax obligations are divinely linked to the function of government (Romans 13:1-7), tax rates should be quite small and never burdensome to a population. High taxes are often the result of wickedness — either of the rulers, or of those ruled, or of both.

The Effects Of High Taxes

Referring to the oppressive taxes that the rulers imposed upon the people of his day, the prophet Micah said,

> *"...Who strip the skin from My people, and the flesh from their bones; who also eat the flesh of My people, flay their skin from them, break their bones, and chop them in pieces like meat for the pot, like flesh in a caldron"* (Micah 3:2-3, NKJV).

Micah's analogy graphically depicted the effects that excessive taxation had upon the people of his day. Rulers were compared to savage cannibals who preyed upon the labor and industry of their people. They took from the people until there was nothing more for them to give but their very lives. We are reminded of the exactions made by Joseph Stalin that caused millions of people to die of starvation. Of course, history is filled with similar cases of abuse; and there are even places today where people suffer to varying degrees under the heavy hand of tyrannical government. The more "enlightened" leaders of modern times have learned that slaves must be made very slowly. The American Revolution demonstrated that people will not tolerate sudden and massive tax increases. The taxes must be increased *gradually* and in subtle and imperceptible ways if they are to be tolerated by society.

By raising taxes gradually over time, governments provide people with time to adjust to the tax, thus making the increase bearable for most people. A survival mechanism kicks in and people simply end up working *more hours* at their job, or *more jobs*, in order to pay their taxes and maintain their accustomed standard of living. They rarely pause to consider just how much of their labor is being siphoned off by their (often) inept, inefficient, and immoral government. Their lives are spent in slavish service to their government. Their freedoms and property are systematically and increasingly confiscated, yet people are conditioned to simply accept this treatment. They are the victims of incrementalism and government-creep. For them, the topic of taxation is merely an unpleasant one. They are not (yet) suffering to the degree of Micah's contemporaries or of Stalin's subjects, so they continue to accept the current levels of taxation (property confiscation) with little or no complaint. Having grown accustomed to the system, they never think to question or challenge it. After all, along with "dying," as the old adage goes, "paying taxes" is something that we just have to do!

While we do have to pay our taxes, it is wrong to assume that government levels of taxation are always right. As noted above, the prophet Micah described a situation in which taxation had become abusive, extortive, and oppressive. He condemned the government officials who so abused their citizens.

Taxation can be so burdensome for many business owners and entrepreneurs that they sometimes wonder why they subject themselves to the added risks, worries, and work that accompany private business ownership. Heavy taxation and government regulations drive some business owners completely out of business. This is sad, for *employees* require *employers*. A healthy economy requires successful business owners. According to Jesus' parable of the *"laborers in the vineyard,"* there had to first be a *vineyard* and a vineyard *owner* before any laborers could be *hired* (Matthew 20:1-16). In order to get started, businesses often need start-up capital and venture capitalists who are willing to invest in their ideas. Jesus described and commended this economic model in the parable of the talents in Matthew 25:14-30.

Some may object to my emphasis upon the physical aspects of these parables. Jesus did have a spiritual mission, and He used parables to teach *spiritual* concepts. However, a "parable" is a truth *alongside* another truth. While Bible teachers and preachers should emphasize the soul-saving principles of parables, we should not ignore the basic economic and practical messages that are also embedded in their stories. Though the soul is of greater value than the flesh (Matthew 16:26) and the preservation of the soul takes precedence over the preservation of the body (Matthew 10:28), we must heartily work to provide for our own sustenance and seek to *"be dependent on no one"* (Colossians 3:23; 1 Thessalonians 4:11-12, ESV). For *"if any would not work, neither should he eat"* (2 Thessalonians 3:10, KJV).

In this study we will learn that safe and productive societies can exist and prosper *without* excessive taxation. We will see that high taxation is *not* God's will for man and is nowhere required by Scripture. The imposition of punitive levels of taxation is a human invention, not a divine invention. As we shall see from 1 Samuel 8, the practice of heavy taxation came as a result of man's *rejection* of God. Heavy taxation was a punishment from God — not a blessing. According to both biblical and secular history, human rulers tend to increase taxes in order to increase their own power and control over other people and to entrench and enrich themselves. It is too often the case that the fruits of human labor are squandered by egomaniacal civil leaders. It does not have to be this way.

To the surprise of some and to the chagrin of others, it is actually *the Bible* that most sensibly and logically addresses the subject of taxation. The Bible presents a reasonable and balanced approach to taxation. It sets forth some good and obvious reasons for paying taxes. At the same time, it limits the scope and size of government, thus also limiting the burden of taxation. The apostle Paul said:

> *"For for this cause you pay tribute also; for they are ministers of God's service, attending continually upon this very thing. Render to all their dues: tribute to whom tribute is due; custom to whom custom; fear to whom fear; honor to whom honor"* (Romans 13:6-7, KJV).

Notice the phrases *"for this cause"* and *"upon this very thing."* These phrases are vital to a correct understanding of God's will with regard to civil taxes. Paul here made a connection between one's duty to pay taxes and the **function** of civil government. Taxes should be paid to support a God-ordained government (Romans 13:1). As defined by the context, a God-ordained government is one that provides a just, safe, and peaceful environment for its citizens. Verses 6 and 7 of Romans 13 can be understood only in the context of verses 3 and 4 of the same chapter:

> *"For rulers are not a terror to good conduct, but to bad. Would you have no fear of the one who is in authority? Then do what is good and you will receive his approval, for he is God's servant* [minister] *for your good. But if you do wrong, be afraid, for he does not bear the sword in vain. For he is the servant of God, an avenger who carries out God's wrath on the wrongdoer"* (Romans 13:3-4, ESV).

The "minister" of verse 4 is the minister(s) of verse 6. These "ministers" are the *powers that be* of verse 1 and the civil *"rulers"* of verse 3 (also Titus 3:1). They are the *"kings"* of 1 Timothy 2:2 and 1 Peter 2:13, the *"governors"* of 1 Peter 2:14, and the *"authorities"* of Titus 3:1. They are civil leaders of varying rank. The God-assigned role of these rulers is to promote the welfare of those who *"do good"* and to punish those who *"do evil."* The apostle Peter made precisely the same point in 1 Peter 2:14. He defined the purpose and function of civil government as being *"to punish those who do evil and praise those who do good."* The fact that this is stated twice, in two different epistles by two different apostles is significant. According to 1 Timothy 2:1-2, one should pray for civil rulers to provide an atmosphere in which he can *"lead a peaceful and quiet life, godly and dignified in every way"* (ESV). It is the role of government to provide a **safe**, **secure**, and **free** environment in which people may freely do the things that God would have them to do and to live the way that God would have them to live. Government helps those who *"do good"* simply by providing *equal justice* and *equal opportunity*. Income redistributionists and socialists desire equality *of outcome,* which is not the same thing. Equality of *opportunity* encourages personal responsibility. Whereas, equality of *outcome* actually *discourages* personal responsibility and places the responsibility for one person's condition upon another person. As referenced before, the Bible teaches that if one will not work, then neither should he eat (2 Thessalonians 3:10). While we are instructed to help those who cannot help themselves (ex. *the Good Samaritan,* Luke 10:30-37), we are not to help capable people who simply refuse to help themselves. Of course, governments do this regularly, which is the main reason for the staggering debts that many countries have amassed. How many of the 47 million Americans currently on food stamps are actually incapable of providing for themselves?

Taxes should be paid to support the government functions that are outlined in the above passages. Government is not to be obeyed or supported when it prevents one from serving and obeying God. According to the apostle Peter, in such cases of conflict and contradiction, *"we must obey God rather than men"* (Acts 5:29; *see also* Acts 4:19-20).

We should pause to consider the ease and simplicity of God's tax plan, particularly in contrast with those that presently exist in many countries today. *(The United States tax code presently contains over 72,000 pages!)* The above passages limit the *size, scope, and function* of civil government. This necessarily limits the amount of tax dollars required to support its function. A God-ordained style of government does not require an exorbitant amount of tax dollars in order to maintain its function. There is absolutely no reason why hard-working and industrious people should have to pay a third to a half of their income in various government taxes and fees. The funding of protection services (national defense, border defense, military, police...etc) and criminal justice systems would place only small fiscal demands upon taxpayers. High taxes are the result of government reach and expansion above and beyond its God-assigned role.

Sadly, few governments respect their God-given function. The natural tendency is for government to grow and expand. Government officials curry favor with people by increasing social services. The Bible teaches people to *be dependent on no one.* Governments often encourage dependence, for dependence translates into control. They also maintain control of people through increased regulation. These practices may help politicians keep their offices, but they come at a huge cost to hard-working taxpayers. Excessive taxation eventually turns "constituents" into "subjects," though, as mentioned before, few taxpayers pause to consider their plight.

Why Does This Happen?

1. **Some people are *statists*.** They like the idea of the government taking control of all social and economic affairs. They are willing to trade certain unalienable rights and freedoms for *"cradle to the grave"* care from their government. Whether socialists or full-blown marxists, the statist prefers central planning over individualism and free-market competition. Most statists are terribly naive. They fail to consider the choice-robbing implications of a government-planned society. Under such systems, people are necessarily assigned jobs that they may not want and moved to locations that they may not like. Of course, for a centrally planned society to function, all "citizens" (subjects) are forced to comply. Personal choice is sacrificed for the betterment of the whole society.

2. **Some people are marxist communists.** Unlike the
naive socialist who assumes that social and
economic decisions can be perpetually made by
communities, the marxist knows, as taught by
Marx and Engels, that once socialism displaces
capitalism, it seamlessly transitions into
communism. The state, under tyrannical leaders,
controls all aspects of society. The young protester
of today with his iPhone in one hand and a
"Communism" sign in the other hand is
dangerously ignorant of what life is really like
under communism. Communist countries allow
no freedom of expression or complaint. Protesters
are summarily killed, imprisoned, or placed in
forced-labor camps. Their utopian dream is
actually a nightmare of slavery and hardship.

3. **Sadly, many religious people have
misconceptions about the nature and role of
government.** This leads them to accept and defend
every government action and decision without
question. Britons once believed in *the divine right of
kings,* which is the doctrine that kings derive their
right to rule directly from God. The British people
began to observe the godless behavior and cruel
actions of so many of the kings, and they
eventually realized that such men could not be
God's divine appointments. And though we don't
hear people advocating this old doctrine today,
some Christians do hold a similar concept of civil
authority. They wrongly see Paul's words in
Romans 13:1 (*governing authorities are ordained of
God*) as suggesting some type of miraculous and
direct divine appointment of specific regimes and
personnel. This misconception leads such people
to be blind servants of the government. They do
not question or challenge governing officials for

fear of displeasing God. This is a dangerous and unscriptural view of civil government (*see Chapter Five: "What God Ordained With Respect To Civil Government"*). Those who hold such a view overlook the fact that the Bible, from "Nimrod" of the book of Genesis to the "great whore" of the book of Revelation, describes and condemns the behavior of dozens of wicked civil rulers and governments. For those whose minds return immediately to Daniel's words that *"the Most High rules in the kingdom of men and gives it to whomever He chooses"* (Daniel 4:25, NKJV), I must point out that Daniel lived under the Jewish *theocracy* of Mosaic Law. The system of religion under Christ is not theocratic, nor is His kingdom physical. We are not under a theocracy today. Let us avoid a position on Romans 13:1 that elevates government to a supernatural, god-like status. As I explained earlier, God ordained the **function** of government, not any specific administration, type of government, or particular personnel. For too many people, government is the first place they look to in times of need and hardship. Rather than look to God's providence (Matthew 6:13), they look to government to *deliver them from evil* and *give them their daily bread.* Far too many people, even in our country, are becoming slavishly dependent upon the government.

Small Taxes Under The Divine Model

The divine model of civil government requires a relatively small amount of taxes to operate because the divine model places government in control only of those things that are beyond the scope of the individual to achieve and control. For example,

Romans 12:17-21 prohibits *individuals* from exacting personal revenge upon others. Instead, God assigned this role to civil government: it is God's *"avenger who brings wrath on the one who practices evil"* (Romans 13:3-4). God's system of a third-party criminal justice system safeguards against the abuses that often accompany the personal administration of "justice." The two extremes are vigilantism and sentimentalism. The vigilante would punish without justice, for he thinks only of retaliation; the sentimentalist would not punish at all, for he thinks only of forgiveness. God's system removes the elements of personal passion and prejudice which often interfere with the administration of true justice. Interestingly, many cultures and societies follow, though some unwittingly, the biblical model of criminal justice.

Along with protection from evil men within the nation, there is also the matter of protection from evil men abroad. A standing and well-equipped army is also beyond the scope of mere individuals to maintain, which is precisely why God has assigned this function to civil government. Even if we were to add other protective and emergency relief agencies, our average individual tax burden would be relatively small.

Large Taxes Under The Human Model

Unlike the divine model of government, human models of government often exact exorbitant amounts of taxes from their citizens. Much of this money is then wasted on foolish programs and projects. Other tax dollars are used to enrich political cronies. Worst of all, some tax dollars are spent on things that are morally reprehensible to the taxpayers. Thomas Jefferson said:

> *"To compel a man to furnish contributions of money for the propagation of opinions which he disbelieves and abhors is sinful and tyrannical."*

Several years ago the Hyde Amendment was passed in order to block taxpayer funds from subsidizing abortion. We have recently learned, however, that huge government grants go each year to the abortion provider, *Planned Parenthood*. Of the over 1.2 million abortions that are performed every year in America, *one in every four* is performed by Planned Parenthood. Those of us who believe in the sanctity of human life do not want our tax dollars being used to fund the killing of innocent human beings. I recently read that a government agency had spent thousands of our tax dollars building a "homoerotic" website. Those of us who oppose homosexuality, pornography, lewdness, and evil desire do not want to pay for websites promoting such behavior. The Pentagon just held a "gay pride" event that celebrated the acceptance of homosexuality in our nation. Many of us do not celebrate homosexuality, and we do not want our tax dollars paying for various "events" and "monuments" in its honor. Sadly, many other examples of government spending on immoral projects could be cited.

While religious people are generally more concerned about their tax dollars being used to fund *immoral* and ungodly practices, there is also the issue of tax dollars simply being wasted. (Of course, let us not forget that *good stewardship* is also a biblical principle, as taught by Jesus in Matthew 24:45.)

Government is wasteful by its very nature. People are rarely restrained in their spending when they are spending *other people's* money. Bureaucrats tend to spend tax money lavishly and foolishly because the money is not their own. Their wasteful use of the money results in no personal cost or loss to themselves. This results in repeated bad investments of tax dollars and funding of outlandish and unnecessary studies, projects, and programs. In fact, politicians often *profit* at the taxpayer's loss. Financial scandals are commonplace in government. James Madison wrote:

> *"The apportionment of taxes on the various descriptions of property is an act which seems to require the most exact impartiality; yet there is, perhaps, no legislative act in which greater opportunity and temptation are given to a predominant party to trample on the rules of justice. Every shilling which they overburden the inferior number is a shilling saved to their own pockets."*

This problem is compounded with the *growth* of government. The larger any government becomes, the more tax dollars it wastes. The words of Solomon prove that bloated bureaucracy is not a new problem:

> *"If you see in a province the oppression of the poor and the violation of justice and righteousness, do not be amazed at the matter, for the high official is watched by a higher, and there are yet higher ones over them"* (Ecclesiastes 5:8, ESV).

This same condition exists in our country today: high officials are watched by higher officials, and there are even *higher* officials over them! The United States government continues to grow and expand, adding layer upon redundant layer of largely inefficient bureaucracy. It has been estimated that there are over 1300 federal agencies and approximately three million federal employees. Tax dollars fund these agencies and pay their employees. Remarkably, rather than being encouraged to *cut* spending, certain funding policies actually encourage agencies to spend money unnecessarily. Left-over funds might suggest to administrators that a particular department needs no funding increase for the next fiscal year, so departments spend money just to get rid of it. No private business could survive that followed such a foolish fiscal model.

Thanks to the internet, people are becoming more and more aware of these abuses and they are raising objections to how their hard-earned tax dollars are being spent. Scandals such as the General Services Administration (GSA)/Las Vegas/Hawaii fiasco are being exposed; and watchdog groups are doing investigative reports that expose government waste, fraud, and abuse. Thankfully, our country has a system by which unscrupulous leaders can be peacefully ousted. When enough people become disgusted with how their money is being misused, they will vent their frustrations at the voting booth.

In an ideal civil environment, taxpayers would fund the functions of government that are divinely authorized. The government would spend money only on those things that are *morally* and *legally* authorized. Most governments have some mechanism for authorizing and allocating funds. In the United States, the Constitution provides Congress with spending authority. However, presidents often spend money by executive fiat; and members of Congress often allocate and spend money on policies that will bolster their reelection. Under such conditions, whole voting blocks of unprincipled people can vote themselves money by electing big social program liberals and socialists to high office. Such symbiotic arrangements can last for decades — at least until the liberal politicians run out of other people's money to spend.

The Tax Duty

After considering the way that many of our tax dollars are spent by the government each year, one might be tempted to simply not pay his taxes. Of course, there are certain legal consequences of tax evasion that no one wishes to face; and there is also the *Bible*. Obviously, not all people believe or accept the Bible; but those who do believe it are conscience-bound to follow its instructions. Along with having a financial obligation to God and the church (1 Corinthians 16:1-2), one's own family (1 Timothy 5:4-8), needy brethren and others (Galatians 6:10; Ephesians 4:28; Luke 10:30-37), one has a financial obligation to civil authorities. Though with certain caveats that will be explained later, the Bible teaches us to pay our taxes. Jesus said, *"Render to Caesar the things that are Caesar's, and to God the things that are God's"* (Matthew 22:21, ESV). As referenced above, Paul also instructed us to pay our taxes — *"render therefore to all their dues: tribute to whom tribute is due; custom to whom custom"* (Romans 13:6,7, KJV). People often cite Matthew 17:24-27 to make this point, but the half-shekel tax was a Jewish tax that was prescribed under the Law of Moses. While there are some instructive principles in the passage, no one today is under Mosaic Law. While Matthew 22:21 and Romans 13 do teach us to pay our taxes, even these passages contain certain defining and mitigating factors that are often overlooked by Bible students and others. The Bible passages that instruct us to pay our taxes are balanced by other Bible passages that limit the *scope and function* of civil government. A lean and *limited* government is an inexpensive government.

As the Bible warns and as history demonstrates, taxation can become so oppressive that it turns free people into actual *slaves*. Rather than government existing to serve and protect responsible people (Romans 13:3-4), people become servants to the government. As we shall see, this was never God's intention. Excessive taxation occurs when the people of a nation reject the God-given role and function of government and begin to construct their own model.

Taxation Under The Old Testament

For Old Testament Jews, paying taxes was a simple and easy task. Under Mosaic Law, every Jewish male 20 years of age and above was to pay an annual census tax of one half shekel. It was a flat tax for all in this group; *"the rich shall not pay more and the poor shall not pay less."* This "half-shekel tax," as it was later known, was to be paid as a ransom for deliverance from Egyptian bondage. The money was to be used for the maintenance of the Tent of Meeting (Exodus 30:11-16). It was later used for the Temple in Jerusalem (2 Chronicles 24:4-14). As seen from Matthew 17:24-27, this tax continued into the days of Jesus when it was called the "Temple tax" (v. 24). On the occasion described in this passage, Jesus did not initially pay the tax, which resulted in the questioning of Peter by the tax collector. Jesus used the occasion to teach a lesson about His true relationship to the Temple. After making His point that His position as *"one greater than the Temple"* exempted Him from the tax, in order to avoid offense He paid the tax for himself and for Peter. Interestingly though, the money that He used was miraculously provided by a fish that Peter was instructed to catch. The fish's mouth contained a *stater* coin, or shekel, which paid the tax for both Jesus and Peter (Matthew 17:27).

Let us remember that the Jews lived under a theocratic form of government. This meant that their social, civil, and spiritual lives were intertwined. Their spiritual law was also their civil law. Along with special offerings of crops and animals, Mosaic Law required a tithe (10%) from the people. God's financial demands of the people were in no way burdensome.

"Give Us A King"

The eighth chapter of 1st Samuel records the historic occasion on which the Jews asked Samuel to appoint them a king *"to judge* [them] *like all the nations"* (1 Sam. 8:5, 6). The request displeased Samuel (and God); but God granted their wish and would use their newly chosen form of government as a means to punish them. God did not take lightly their having rejected Him as their King (v. 7); but rather than punish the perpetrators by some direct action, He chose to punish them through their own foolish and ill-conceived desires. Samuel was told to explain to the people the physical demands that would be placed upon them by the monarchical style of government that they so desired:

- The king would conscript their sons into military service.
- Others would be placed into forced labor for the production of food and military equipment.
- Their daughters would be conscripted as perfumers, cooks, and bakers.
- The best of their fields, vineyards, and olive groves would be confiscated and given to the king's officials and attendants.
- Their servants and the best of their cattle and donkeys would be confiscated for the king's own use.
- A 10% tax would be imposed upon their grain, vintage, and flocks (that is, on what remained after the confiscations of the "best" had occurred).
- Samuel concluded his warning with the ominous words, *"And you shall be his slaves"* (1 Samuel 8:17, ESV).

Sadly, even after these plain warnings, the Jews of Samuel's day remained steadfast in their desire for a king, so God gave them Saul. Their dream of a monarchical utopia soon became a nightmare.

Taxation Under Solomon

God's warnings were fully realized by the Jews under the reign of Solomon. The tax burden was so high that upon his death the people assembled before Solomon's son, Rehoboam, and said, *"Your father made our yoke heavy. Now therefore lighten the hard service* of *your father and his **heavy yoke** on us, and we will serve you"* (1 Kings 12:4, ESV). They had reference to the heavy cost of maintaining the king and his administrators. As we shall see, "exploded bureaucracies" are nothing new! King Solomon had thousands of administrators. 3300 are mentioned just in connection with the work of material acquisitions for the Temple (1 Kings 5:16).

Solomon appointed 12 officers to oversee the daily provisions for people and livestock (1 Kings 4:7-19). Each one made provisions for one month of the year. According to 1 Kings 4:22-23, the following provisions were required for *each day* for King Solomon's table:

- 180 bushels of fine flour,
- 360 bushels of meal,
- 10 fat oxen,
- 20 pasture-fed cattle,
- 100 sheep,
- Miscellaneous deer, gazelles, roebucks, and fattened fowl.

Solomon also had 40,000 horses for his chariots, which also had to be fed barley and straw each day. Of course, this list did not include all of the tribute that was paid to Solomon each year by subordinate nations. Solomon eventually accumulated so much gold that silver became worthless (1 Kings 10:21).

Solomon did oversee a vast empire (1 Kings 4:21), requiring numerous aides and administrators. It could be argued that these sizable quantities of daily provisions were a necessary expense. However, let us remember God's warning that human kings and kingdoms would *create* such needs and would then require the services of Jewish sons and daughters to supply those needs. This has generally been the practice of human governments ever since.

The Power To Tax Is The Power To Enslave

1 Kings 5:13 tells us that Solomon *"drafted forced labor out of all Israel, and the draft numbered 30,000 men"* (ESV). He also appointed 70,000 burden-bearers and 80,000 stone-cutters. 3300 officers were required to oversee these laborers. Any government with the power to force its citizens to give up their wealth and property also has the power to force its citizens into slavery. Of course, Samuel warned the people that these conditions would exist under monarchical government. He told the people, **"You shall be his slaves"** (1 Samuel 8:17, ESV). That is precisely what happened.

There is a great lesson in the fact that Solomon was not an *evil* king. He *"loved the Lord, walking in the statutes of his father David"* and was blessed by God with great wisdom and understanding (1 Kings 3:3; 4:29). Even so, his reign placed tremendous hardships upon his people. We learn from Solomon's example that the kingdoms of even *good* kings place a terrible burden upon the citizens who are expected to maintain them. Solomon took from the strength and substance of the people whatever was required to fuel government expansion. As noted above, human governments become a vast labyrinth of administrations, agencies, and offices that are expensive to maintain. Interestingly, *it was Solomon himself* who described the inefficient and oppressive monstrosity that government often becomes:

> *"If you see in a province the oppression of the poor and the violation of justice and righteousness, do not be amazed at the matter, for **the high official is watched by a higher, and there are yet higher ones over them**"* (Ecclesiastes 5:8, ESV).

Such is the nature of human government — layer upon wasteful layer of inefficient redundancy. Under the Jewish *theocracy,* with God as their only "King," the primary function of the people was to serve God; and His requirements are never *"grievous"* (1 John 5:3, KJV). Prior to the kings, no vast bureaucracies existed among the Jews to siphon off the fruits of their labor and break their entrepreneurial spirits. Heavy taxation and despair happened because of the impositions of *human* government. The same thing happens today.

Taxation Under Other Kings

Samuel's warnings extended beyond the era of the United Kingdom and into the era of the Divided Kingdom. Amos told the leaders of his day:

> *"Therefore, because you tread down the poor and take* ***grain taxes*** *from him, though you have built houses of hewn stone, yet you shall not dwell in them; you have planted pleasant vineyards, but you shall not drink wine from them"* (Amos 5:11, NKJV).

Through taxation, the poor were *"tread down;"* and government officials lived sumptuously. So commonplace were these taxes that Amos made incidental mention of *"the king's mowings"* in Amos 7:1. This had reference to a tax that was imposed upon all farmers. It was an Old Testament example of the tax *incrementalism* that was mentioned earlier. God had nowhere required or authorized this tax. It was imposed upon the people, and they grew to simply accept it. This type of thing is done constantly by human governments. In low growth years, the farmers may not have had much to live on; but the government always received their exactions of grain. Thomas Paine wrote:

"Invention is continually exercised, to furnish new pretenses for revenues and taxation. It watches prosperity as its prey and permits none to escape without tribute" (Rights of Man, 1791).

The taxes described by Amos were not merely the typical and fair costs of conducting business in the land. They were excessive and oppressive. As is typically the case, the taxpayers funded the extravagant and luxurious lifestyles of the ruling class. Amos had earlier criticized the wives of the leaders, saying:

"Hear this word, you cows of Bashan who are on the mountain of Samaria, who oppress the poor, who crush the needy, who say to your husbands, 'Bring now, that we may drink'" (Amos 4:1).

We are reminded of political elites who take lavish vacations at taxpayer expense. Oppressive taxation impoverished the taxpayers while enriching the ruling class. Amos said they *"lie upon beds of ivory, and stretch themselves upon their couches, and eat the lambs out of the flock, and the calves out of the midst of the stall"* (Amos 6:4, KJV). In other words, they lived lives of unrestrained luxury and did so upon the backs of those who were forced by human law to support them. This was not God's original purpose for man. Man entered this abysmal condition of governance due to his own carnal desire to "be like the other nations." Since those days millions of people all over the world have found themselves in similar circumstances.

Things have not changed much since Amos' day. A recent study revealed that the *richest* counties in the United States are those in and around Washington, D. C. We have lately seen news reports of videos of government workers partying luxuriously on taxpayer dollars. "Crony capitalism" has resulted in billions of taxpayer funds propping up corporations with friendly ties to the government (Fannie Mae, Freddie Mac, General Motors,

Chrysler, Solyndra, Ener1, Abound Solar, Solar Trust, and dozens of other government-backed green energy companies). The corporate executives of these companies have been enriched at the taxpayers' expense.

As mentioned above, Micah described in graphic detail the effects of high levels of taxation on the people of his day. Speaking of the "unjust" rulers he said:

> "...Who strip the skin from my people, and the flesh from their bones; who also eat the flesh of my people, flay their skin from them, break their bones, and chop them in pieces like meat for the pot, like flesh in a caldron" (Micah 3:2-3, NKJV).

This metaphor powerfully describes the effects of excessive taxation. Taxpayers are pictured as the helpless victims of savage and brutal treatment by others. These rulers were worse than vicious animals — they were vicious *cannibals:* they tore the flesh from the people's bones, chopped it up, and boiled it in a caldron for their own consumption. The lesson is powerful and clear: excessive taxation takes more than just people's property — it destroys their very *lives.* It drains people of their incentives and aspirations. It dampens and even destroys the entrepreneurial spirit.

It is interesting to observe that even in God's *punishment* of Adam (man), God's treatment of man was less financially demanding of him than the tax schemes of many human governments today. In pronouncing His curse upon Adam, God told him that he would have to obtain his food through *pain* and *sweat* (Genesis 3:17, 19). Under God's punishment, the degree of labor difficulty was increased for Adam. However, Adam was at least allowed the use and ownership of the fruits of his labor. As we have seen, this has not been the case under human government. Under the tax codes of many countries today, the longer, harder, and smarter that one works, the more money the government takes from him.

Though there were some good kings among the Jews of the Old Testament, many people suffered immensely under the monarchical system. Their royal monarchy began badly and ended even worse. The kingship of their first king, Saul, ended with his shameful suicide (1 Samuel 31:4). The kingship of their last king, Zedekiah, ended when Babylonian soldiers killed his sons before his very eyes, then blinded him, placed him in bronze shackles, and led him into Babylonian captivity (2 Kings 25:7). Their confidence in their kings sapped Israel and Judah of their physical and financial resources and led them into sin and subsequent captivities.

The Slavery of Income Redistributionism

We have recently seen a sharp rise in redistributionism chatter. *Income redistribution* is the doctrine that it is the role of government to confiscate wealth from one class of citizens and give it to another. The money is exacted through tax policies that target the rich and so-called "rich." This policy fuels envy and class warfare, which is then used to motivate voters. The policy ignores the fact that we have already had a graduated tax code in the United States for years and that roughly 90% of all federal taxes are are paid by 10% of the people. The doctrine is actually socialistic; but jealous and envious people do not think rationally, and thus they ignore the long-term psychological and economical impact of their ideology upon society. They think only of "equality" of outcome and of the "rich paying their fair share." They think only of punishing those who have acquired more than themselves. They do not consider that some people simply work harder, smarter, and/or longer than other people and are financially rewarded for their efforts.

In His *parable of the talents* (Matthew 25:14-30), Jesus rejected the practice of income redistribution. In the parable, a traveling businessman dispersed investment funds (a "talent" was a monetary unit) to three employees according to their differing abilities. One was given five talents, another two, and another one. The five and two-talent men doubled their employer's investment and they were commended for their efforts. The one-talent man buried his master's money, and he was later condemned for his unprofitableness. Interestingly, the Lord commanded that the one talent be taken from him and given to the five-talent man. This is quite contrary to the redistributionist's policy, for redistributionists would have taken a percentage of wealth from the two talent man, and a greater percentage from the five talent man, and then given that money to the one talent man in an effort to achieve parity. Obviously, Jesus was not as "politically correct" as some are today. Nor was Jesus a socialist.

The redistributionist policy makes slaves of both the "haves" and the "have-nots." The "have-nots" or "takers" are enslaved to the government due to their dependence upon it for their sustenance. The "haves" or "givers" are enslaved to the government through a punitive tax code. Both are enslaved to a system that refuses to acknowledge personal responsibility and personal liberty.

It should be observed that government has only the powers that are given to it by the governed. As explained before, God does not "ordain" government in the sense of direct divine appointment. God made men free agents, and He allows them to exercise that free agency in their selection of their leaders. As the old adage goes, people really do deserve the government that they elect. The problem is that too many people stand quite ready to cede their fates and the control of their lives into the hands of their civil leaders. Like the Jews of old, many even in our country today stand ready to enslave themselves to government. So much do they despise personal responsibility that they would sell their liberty to purchase a little security. Such people, as Benjamin Franklin said, *"deserve neither liberty nor security."*

Scriptural Principles Of Taxation

As explained above, civil government is not "ordained" in the sense of direct divine appointment of specific personnel, regimes, or government types. What God ordained was the *function* of civil government (Romans 13:1-4; 1 Peter 2:13-14). Taxes are to be paid to support these prescribed functions (Romans 13:6-7).

This, of course, begs a serious question: what if one's government does not adhere to this God-given model? What if it squanders money, or worse, uses it for immoral purposes? Are people morally obligated to support such governments? The Bible teaches that government should provide a "peaceful" environment for those who "do good" and who lead "godly and dignified" lives. Government is to punish those who are disruptive and "evil." What if a government enacts policies that actually punish those who are peaceable and responsible and rewards those who do evil? Should such a government be funded? Let us take this a step further: what about a government that decides to practice forced abortion and infanticide in order to control its population? Should taxpayers fund such policies? What if it decides to implement a policy of euthanasia in an effort to eliminate citizens whom it deems too "unproductive" to remain in society? Should its "productive" citizens pay tax dollars in order to fund the executions of its "unproductive" citizens? What about governments like those of Mao, Stalin, and Hitler, which slaughtered millions of innocent people in the name of "ethnic cleansing" or political reformation? Would Romans 13 obligate Christians to pay taxes in support of their murderous policies? Obviously not. Just a couple of verses after the tax mandate of Romans 13:6-7, Paul condemned the practice of *murder* (Romans 13:9). Furthermore, Romans 1:32 teaches that those who approve and encourage sinful behavior are just as guilty of that behavior as are those who actually commit the behavior (see also this principle in 2 John 10-11).

Practices like forced abortion, euthanasia, and ethnic cleansing may seem like extreme examples to cite for the above point. However, these things are actually happening in some countries even today. And let us remember that *even in this country,* since Roe V. Wade, over 50,000,000 unborn babies have been deliberately and "legally" aborted. The question of government evil is worthy of our careful consideration. Obviously, good judgment must be used when making decisions about what is the best way to handle such evils. *A reminder: the ballot box is always better than the bullet box.* When government evils abound, people should speak out; and they should vote.

Answering Some Objections

The unreligious have no concerns about God or His Scriptures. They make their judgments about the size, scope, nature, and operation of government on purely human terms. However, as is demonstrated throughout this chapter, those of us who *are* Bible believers are conscience-bound to respect its teaching on all subjects — including that of the role of civil government. Of course, we are obligated to "handle" the Scriptures accurately (2 Timothy 2:15), speaking only *"as the oracles of God"* (1 Peter 4:11, KJV). Those who twist the Scriptures do so to *"their own destruction"* (2 Peter 3:16), so it is critical that we interpret and explain Scripture honestly and accurately.

Of course, we do not *always* correctly understand *all* Bible passages. We can make mistakes in our own analysis, or we can be misled by others. People often approach the Bible with faulty preconceptions. Some people fail to observe basic interpretive rules: they ignore the context or misdefine terms. Many people make the mistake of conflating various dispensations — they mix various requirements of Mosaic Law with the gospel of Christ or Patriarchal law. This section will briefly address some of these misconceptions as they relate to the question of the God-assigned role and function of civil government.

Romans 13:5: This passage is sometimes cited in an effort to prove that Christians (and others) should support and fund even evil governments in order to satisfy their consciences. This is not what the passage teaches. The apostle Paul said,

> *"Therefore one must be in subjection, not only to avoid God's wrath but also for the sake of conscience"* (ESV).

The apostle was not telling people to obey and fund the government regardless of what it did: he is telling saints *why* they are to "be in subjection." The expression "to avoid God's wrath" relates back to the previous verse where Paul described civil authority as the "minister" of God's wrath. One reason for obeying civil law is to avoid being punished. The expression "for the sake of conscience" relates back to verse 1 where Paul said that civil authority is "ordained" of God. Thus, not only does the Christian wish to avoid civil punishment, he also wishes to please God. He wishes to have a good conscience toward God (1 Peter 2:19).

Let us remember that Paul has already defined the function of civil government as being **for good** and **against evil**. To argue from this passage that we are "conscience-bound" to support and fund wholesale evil (provided that it is done by government) is laughable.

1. Moses' parents were not "conscience-bound" to surrender Moses to Pharaoh to be killed (Exodus 2). On the contrary, they acted *"by faith"* when

they protected Moses from Pharaoh's infanticide policy (Hebrews 11:23).

2. Rahab was not "conscience-bound" to turn Joshua's spies over to Jericho authorities. She acted "by faith" when she hid them from their enemies (Joshua 2; Hebrews 11:31); and she and her family members were later saved from Jericho's destruction (Joshua 7).

3. Shadrach, Meshach, and Abed-nego were not "conscience-bound" to obey Nebuchadnezzar's order for them to worship the golden image. On the contrary, they were miraculously protected and saved by God. One "like the Son of Man" miraculously visited them in the burning furnace (Daniel 3)!

4. Daniel was not "conscience-bound" to obey the government's no-prayer policy. He also was miraculously protected by God (Daniel 6).

5. Joseph and Mary were not "conscience-bound" to surrender Jesus to Herod for execution. They obeyed God by fleeing to Egypt (Matthew 2:13-15).

6. Peter and the other apostles were not "conscience-bound" to obey the edict of the Sanhedrin that they stop preaching the gospel. Instead, they said *"we must obey God rather than men"* (Acts 4:19-20; 5:29).

7. The disciples at Damascus were not "conscience-bound" to reveal Paul's location to city officials who were trying to apprehend him. They instead helped him to escape (Acts 9:25).

"The laws of nature are the laws of God, whose authority can be superseded by no power on earth. A legislature must not obstruct our obedience to Him, from whose punishment they cannot protect us. All human

laws which contradict His laws we are in conscience bound to disobey." (James Madison)

Other examples could be cited, but these suffice to make the point. The Bible NOWHERE assigns such a role to conscience. We are never "conscience-bound" to support evil.

Romans 13:6-7: This passage (already quoted above) is used to argue that since Paul commanded the Christians in Rome to pay their taxes *even though the Roman government was killing innocent people and engaging in other immoralities and atrocities,* then we must support and fund wicked governments today. While this argument sounds plausible, it overlooks certain facts and extenuating circumstances:

1. The argument assumes that the Roman government fits the paradigm of a *God-ordained* government, *which it did not.* As noted above, Paul instructs saints to pay taxes to governments that "attend upon" the tasks of *punishing evildoers* and *protecting those who do what is right* (Romans 13:3-7). The Roman government (eventually) had leaders who tortured and slaughtered God's people. Some of its emperors were worshipped as "gods." These were not the functions of a God-ordained government, but of an *anti-God* government. God killed Herod for accepting praise as God (Acts 12:22-23). One should not take a position on taxes that would have required the Christians of Nero's day to pay for the tar, bindings, and stakes that were used by Nero to bind and burn Christians to death! No Bible passage requires Christians to fund the perverted pleasures of psychopathic leaders. This argument ignores the context of Romans 13.

2. The argument also ignores the fact that Rome's

downfall was being divinely orchestrated even as Paul penned the Roman epistle. We know this only because of Daniel's prophecy in the second chapter of Daniel. *[Incidentally, Bible teachers should be very careful about making claims about how God uses nations and governments today. In the absence of specific revelation, such claims are mere speculation.]* According to Daniel's explanation of the "great image" of Nebuchadnezzar's dream, Rome was the fourth and final world empire. There would be no more physical *world* empires. The *spiritual* kingdom of the church would *"break in pieces and consume"* all prior kingdoms, including the Roman kingdom; and the Lord's spiritual kingdom would then stand forever (Dan. 2:44, 45). After blowing his trumpet, the seventh angel of Revelation proclaimed, *"The kingdom of the world has become the kingdom of our Lord and of His Christ; and He will reign forever and ever"* (Revelation 11:15). Being in the purview of Daniel's prophecy and being marked by God as the final world empire, the Roman Empire held a special place among world governments. It had been divinely designated as the kingdom in power at the time of the establishment of God's eternal kingdom, and it was divinely designated for destruction.

In addition to the role of divine fiat in Rome's demise, there is also the divine *providence* of what God has *provided* in creation and in human nature. The liberating principles of the gospel message are counteractive to the designs of totalitarian regimes. By designing humans as *free agents,* God designed humans to desire and appreciate *freedom.* One cannot say "free agency" with saying "free." By divine design, humans aspire to be free. Their aspirations may be occasionally doused by tyrannical oversight and abusive taxation, but the spark of freedom nonetheless remains. People will take advantage of any opportunity to reacquire their freedom. Interestingly, the more that people are exposed to the principles of the gospel, the more they appreciate basic liberty, and the less tolerant they are of tyranny. It should be no surprise that George Washington and many other revolutionaries of the early Revolutionary movement were avid readers and believers of the Bible. As such, they had keen insights into the principle of liberty. They risked and gave their lives in the maintenance of freedom.

3. As noted before, certain Roman emperors did some evil things. However, the Roman Empire also did *some* good things. It built roads, improved sea travel, established a common language, and maintained societal order — all of which facilitated in the spread of the gospel. If an argument can be made from Romans 13 that we are to pay taxes even to evil governments, the argument must be that our taxes are devoted for good and authorized uses, not for evil. It must be that even though a government may generally follow the divine model, yet its leaders may sometimes behave counter to that design. Obviously, funds are *fungible,* which means that we often have no control over the actual use of our tax dollars. However, Paul's idol-meat-purchase principle of 1 Corinthians 10:25 (see also 1 Corinthians 8:4-ff.) does show that one can pay for a product or service *without* necessarily endorsing all of the provider's views and conduct. One can purchase a good product or service from a bad person. Of course, as was mentioned under point

1 above, the situation becomes intolerable when a government engages in deadly atrocities. Murder, unpunished by society, can only be expiated by the death of that society.

The gospel message is a message of *"liberty"* (Isaiah 61:1). While the primary focus of this message is freedom from *sin*, the actual "proclaiming" of that message requires *freedom of expression*. It should be noted that it was not the Romans but the *Jews* who banned gospel preaching (Acts 4:18; 5:28). The acceptance of the gospel message requires *freedom of thought* and *action*. These freedoms were exercised freely throughout the Roman Empire. In Paul's day, Athens was known for its open exchanges of thoughts and ideas (Acts 17:21). Paul's troubles with Roman authorities were often the result of complaints from Jews and idolaters (Acts 16 & 19), not because of conflicts with any Roman law. Ephesus city officials were concerned about a "riot," not about the substance of Paul's teaching (Acts 19:37,40). When Jesus commissioned the apostles to take the gospel into "all the world" (Mk. 16:15), He assumed their *freedom of movement* from place to place. As demonstrated in the four Gospels and in the book of Acts, under Roman rule, both Jesus and the apostles had considerable freedom of movement.

For these reasons, I advise caution when citing the moral conditions of first century Rome as proof that one must *always* pay his taxes regardless of government conduct. Islamic Sharia compliant governments openly and actively seek to banish all Bibles and kill all Christians. Such governments should not be supported by saints.

Matthew 22:21: Jesus said, *"Render to Caesar the things that are Caesar's; and to God the things that are God's."* Jesus made a distinction between two completely different and often-conflicting realms of activity — human law and divine law. Many people cite this passage in an effort to prove that people are to pay taxes in support of their government regardless of how godless its policies. This view pits Scripture against Scripture, for Romans 13 tells saints to pay taxes so that the government can *punish evildoers* and *praise those who do what is right.* Though God condemns murder, they would have Matthew 22:21 obligating saints to fund things like **abortion, infanticide, and euthanasia.** They have obviously misapplied and overextended the passage.

In Matthew 22:17-21, Jesus answered the tax question by pointing out that currency belongs to the organization (government) that prints it. Roman currency contained Caesar's image and superscription because it was minted by the Roman government. For this reason Jesus instructed people to render unto Caesar *"the things"* that are Caesar's. Jesus had reference to the *currency* or *coinage* that contained his image. The government that prints or mints the currency has the power also to regulate, control, and even confiscate that currency. Gold was confiscated in the United States under the Roosevelt Act of 1933. In rendering to Caesar *"the things that are Caesar's,"* one is paying the government for the right to participate in its currency system. While this system makes doing business with others easier than under a barter system, it also places most revenue under government control, regulation, and taxation. History does prove that as taxes increase, so does barter.

The danger in the view that some have of Matthew 22:21 is in assuming Jesus was implying some God-given power of government to control one's personal life and labor. Jesus teaches no such thing. He grants the government control only of the currency that it mints. The Bible teaches that just as no man is the automatic property of other men, neither is his labor the automatic property of other men. That one's labor is his own property is clearly established by the following passages:

- Genesis 3:17-19 describes God's punishment of Adam because of his sin. Eden had provided a perfect living environment, but Adam and Eve's sin resulted in their being cast out of Eden. Outside of Eden, Adam would have to produce his food through *pain* and *sweat*. Though far more difficult to obtain than in Eden, the food that Adam harvested and produced was nonetheless *his* to use for himself and his family. God granted Adam ownership of the food that he produced through his own labor.
- Acts 5:1-4 describes the sin of Ananias and Sapphira. We are told that they sold property and donated part of the price to the church. This would have been fine, but they lied about the percentage of their giving. Their sin was not in giving only part of their property proceeds to the church; it was in their *lying* about the percentage. Peter told them that the property, prior to the sale, was *theirs to use as they pleased*. He also told them that the proceeds following the sale were theirs to use as they pleased. We learn from Peter that God allowed them *private ownership of their property* and control of their own money. By a direct statement of an inspired apostle, we know that people have a God-given right to the fruits of their labor. *[Incidentally, along with the parable of the talents and other Bible teaching, this passage refutes the concept of socialism.]*
- James 4:13 describes free market economy in a nutshell. With the motive of making *"a profit,"* the businessman decided the *type of business* that he would conduct, the *place* he would go to conduct that business, and *how long* he would stay there. James condemns none of these elements of free

market economy. He condemns only the godless attitude of one who fails to acknowledge God in the course of his business pursuits. According to this passage, a person's profits are *his own*. The biblical principle is clear: though one's body and spirit are God's with respect to their spiritual use and purpose (1 Corinthians 6:20), God allows each person control over his own body and ownership of the fruits of his own labor. In telling us to render to Caesar the things that are Caesars, Jesus does not negate this principle.

Often overlooked is the second half of the Lord's instructions in Matthew 22:21: we are to (render) *"to God the things that are God's."* Under the levels of taxation described in passages like Micah 3, people had little or no ability to fulfill their financial obligations to God. In the time of Micah under the Law of Moses, the people were to pay a tenth of their income to God *(additional offerings were made of various sacrifices of first fruits of animals and grains)*. Under the Law of Christ, people are to contribute upon the first day of every week *"as he may prosper"* (1 Corinthians 16:1-2). The Bible also teaches that men have the responsibility to *"provide"* for the physical well-being of their families (1 Timothy 5:8) and help others as they are able (Ephesians 4:28; Galatians 6:10). Parents are to *"save up...for their children"* (2 Corinthians 12:14); then later, children are to *"make some return to their parents"* (1 Timothy 5:4). Excessive taxation prevents people from fulfilling their God-given financial obligations. The tax-paying instructions of Jesus in Matthew 22:21 should not be interpreted in a way that negates these other obligations that are "rendered" either "to God" or in accordance with God's will.

Matthew 17:24-27 is cited as a tax obligation passage. However, as noted above, this passage has reference to the Exodus 30 half-shekel Tabernacle/Temple tax of Mosaic Law;

and it has no application today. We are today "under law to Christ," not Moses (1 Corinthians 9:21; Galatians 6:2; John 1:17). The Jewish Temple was destroyed by the Romans in 70 A.D., and the Law of Moses was abolished by the death of Christ (Colossians 2:14; 2 Corinthians 3:13, 14; Ephesians 2:14, 15). We are no more under the Temple tax law than we are the Old Testament animal sacrifice laws or the Levitical priesthood. Furthermore, unlike the theocratic system of governance under Mosaic Law, the religion of Christ does not combine spiritual and civil governance. Christ is King over a *spiritual* kingdom. His kingdom *"is not of this world"* (John 18:36; Luke 17:20, 21). It is a misuse of Scripture to apply Matthew 17:24-27 to modern day civil tax obligations and procedures.

"Lest We Offend"

Still, some would like to at least make a principle application of the *"lest we offend"* phrase in Matthew 17:27. Jesus said, *"Nevertheless, lest we offend them, go to the sea, cast in a hook, and take the fish that comes up first. And when you have opened his mouth, you will find a piece of money; take that and give it to them for Me and you"* (Matthew 17:27, NKJV).

Some argue from this passage that we should pay our taxes only in order to avoid offending others. Some invoke this principle on the basis that Christians are actually members of Christ's *spiritual kingdom,* with Christ as their king, and thus have no connection to human government (they don't vote or participate in government in any way). Others invoke the principle as an excuse to continue paying taxes to a godless government. The principle works for neither one. One does not "avoid offense" by funding what he deems to be sinful and wrong.

As explained earlier in the chapter, Jesus held a unique position with respect to the Temple — as God, He was *"greater"* than the Temple (Matthew 12:6). Some did not know Jesus' real identity and might have concluded that He was avoiding fulfilling a divine obligation. Rather than provide an opportunity for accusation, Jesus simply paid the tax.

For the lest-we-offend claim to be analogous today, taxpayers would have to be exempt from taxation but paying taxes only to avoid offending tax-collectors. However, according to Romans 13:6-7 we are not exempt from paying our taxes and are in fact obligated to pay taxes in support of a God-ordained government. The "lest we offend" provision does not apply in this connection.

Genesis 47 is often cited as a model of taxation. We are told that Joseph imposed a 20% flat tax on the Egyptians in exchange for the state giving them seed-grain. One preacher became somewhat famous as a result of a sermon that he preached on Joseph's tax. For about two years I repeatedly received a particular (viral) email that touted this story of Joseph's flat tax. I must say that I am not quite as enthused about a 20% federal tax rate as some others appear to be:

1. I wrote earlier in this article of the ill-effects of incrementalism. Taxes are raised to crippling levels and people accept them only because the increases have occurred gradually over time. Conditions have greatly degenerated in this country when people begin to think of a 20% national tax as *a good thing!* Have they forgotten about all of the other taxes that must be paid? If implemented, **this 20% national tax would be in addition to** *state and local income taxes, school tax, sales tax, social security, medicare and medicaid taxes, federal and state unemployment taxes, property and real estate taxes, fuel tax, vehicle registration tax, multiple*

federal, state and local telephone taxes, **and dozens of other special, recreational, corporate, and commercial taxes.** The present national average of federal tax is approximately 18%. A 20% federal tax rate would actually be an average increase for taxpaying Americans. Combined with all of the other taxes (and fees), the average American taxpayer already pays close to 50% of his income in taxes. *[Note: There is a difference between the phrase "average American" and "average American taxpayer." Some estimate the tax for the "average American" at 30%, and the rate for "above average taxpayers" at 57%.]* This rate of taxation is simply too high. God never intended for tax rates under Egyptian nationalism to serve as a model for governments today. This leads to the next point.

2. As described in Genesis 47, the drought, which affected both Canaan and Egypt, had forced the people to use all of their money to buy government grain. When their funds were depleted they traded their livestock for grain. When their livestock were gone they traded their land for grain. All of the land was nationalized under Pharaoh. At that point the people became *"servants"* (slaves) of the state (Genesis 47:21, ESV). A deal was made in which the state gave them annual allotments of seed-grain in exchange for a 20% return of their harvested grain. The real story of Genesis 47 is one of *statism* and *nationalism.* All it took was 7 years of famine to turn free people into slaves to the state. The book of Genesis ends with the Egyptian people under this arrangement. The book of Exodus opens with the rise of a new Pharaoh who was unfamiliar with Joseph. His policies also turned the Jews into slaves, hence the term "Egyptian bondage." The

power to tax is the power to enslave.

3. As noted earlier, once the Jews left Egypt and received their own law (Mosaic), they were under no such "20%" national tax law. The half-shekel tax was far shy of 20%, and tithe was only one half of it. The practice of "tithing" actually predated Egypt (Genesis 14:20).

Though it does provide us with proof that godliness, like that possessed by Joseph, can help to mitigate against government tyranny, Genesis 47 provides no model for government or taxation. We must be careful in our use of this passage. Were we in a civil arrangement in which we had no other taxes and fees to pay, a 20% flat tax might sound appealing. But under federalism, with multi-tier government and taxation, it would actually be far more burdensome than what many people presently pay.

Conclusion

Some civil leaders are conscientious people who care for their constituents. However, some civil leaders use taxation as a means of empowering themselves and subjugating others, acquiring fame and popularity, funding their own lavish lifestyles and self-aggrandizing adventures, and advancing their own selfish ambitions and agendas. It is not a pretty picture, but it is sadly the history of human government. God never intended for humans to be robbed and abused by their civil rulers, but He does allow them to make their own foolish choices. When Old Testament Jews rejected God's leadership and clamored for "a king" to make them like the other nations, God gave them a king. The Jews were repeatedly burdened under that arrangement, and people continue to be burdened under the weight of anti-God government today. The Bible provides a model for civil government that places only small tax demands upon citizens. Taxation does not have to be burdensome, but it will be burdensome as long as governments continue to operate beyond the scope of their God-ordained function.

11

WHY CHRISTIANS SHOULD VOTE

Democratically elected representatives and officials make decisions that have a tremendous impact upon our lives. They have the power to pass laws; impose rules, regulations, and taxes; and appoint judges. Their decisions can either shape civil government after the divine model that is revealed in Scripture (Romans 13:1-10), or they can shape it after the model of the "sea beast" and the "great whore" of the Apocalypse — an intrusive, abusive, and invasive government that was both anti-God and anti-man (Revelation 13, 17, 18). Considering how much power politicians have to affect our lives, either for the better or for the worse, it behooves us to do all that we can to elect honorable ones. In a democracy, the voting booth is where one makes his strongest statement.

Two Models of Government

The Bible describes two models of government: one that is "ordained" of God, and one that is of the Devil. The *divine model* of government operates in the best interests of the governed (Romans 13:1-10; 1 Peter 2:13-15; 1 Timothy 2:1, 2). Its legislators make decisions and pass laws that are consistent with the great biblical principles contained in the second commandment (the **"Royal Law"** — James 2:8) and the **Golden Rule**: *loving one's neighbor as oneself* (doing him no harm) and *treating others as one wishes to be treated* (Romans 13:9, 10; Matthew 7:12).

The divine model of government promotes and preserves the peace, safety, and security of its citizens. It provides an atmosphere in which citizens *"may lead...quiet and peaceable* [lives] *in all godliness and honesty"* (1 Timothy 2:2, KJV). It cultivates a climate of personal responsibility in which people are free to do *"honest work with [their] own hands"* (Ephesians 4:28, ESV) and pursue their own ambitions as Paul instructed the Thessalonians: *"Make it your ambition to lead a quiet life and attend to your own business and work with your hands..."* (1 Thessalonians 4:11). According to James 4:13, it is a government that provides for **free market capitalism** — an environment in which people are free to make their own decisions about *where* they do business ("such and such a city"), *how much time* they spend at that business ("continue there a year"), *how they do business* ("buy and sell"), and as a result of their efforts, *"make a profit."* As clearly illustrated by Jesus in the parable of the talents (Matthew 25:14-30), the form of economy advocated in the Bible is capitalism, not socialism or communism.

The other is *Satan's model* of government. It is characterized by *self-interest* and the attainment of *power, control,* and *wealth.* It is this model that is being followed when legislators make decisions and pass laws that serve only to empower and enrich themselves and their cronies. Rather than *punish evil people,* as done by God-ordained government (1 Peter 2:14), such governments excuse and even reward evildoers. Rather than praise, protect, and support good and responsible people, this model of government actually punishes them! This is usually done through punitive levels of taxation, but history repeatedly demonstrates that it is often done by persecution and even slaughter.

It is important to note that both Bible and secular history show that either model can be pursued regardless of the *type* of government, whether a *monarchy, democracy,* or *oligarchy.* For example, the books of the Kings describe some of the Jewish kings as doing what was "right" and others as doing what was "wrong." Solomon described the ideal king: *"A king who sits on the throne of justice disperses all evil with his eyes"* (Proverbs 20:8). Regardless of the type of government or kind of governmental officials (kings, governors, or elected representatives), Christians should support those who will work for the divine model of government.

Understanding the difference between these two models of government makes the Bible student the best voter. His vote is cast, not on the basis of a candidate's appearance or charisma, but upon the basis of bedrock biblical principles. He knows that *"righteousness exalts a nation"* and that *"sin is a disgrace to any people"* (Proverbs 14:34). He knows that the *"throne is established on righteousness"* (Proverbs 16:12; 25:5).

Some wrongly conclude that referencing such Old Testament Scriptures constitutes a call for a *theocracy.* While it is true that Solomon lived and wrote under a theocratic form of government [God was the true King of Israel], "righteousness" does not "exalt a nation" *only in a theocracy.* "Righteousness" involves the right treatment of others and can be practiced in any type of government and in any age or country. While discussing *civil government* (Romans 13:1-10), Paul said, *"The commandments, 'You shall not commit adultery, You shall not murder, You shall not steal, You shall not covet,' and any other commandment, are summed up on this word: 'You shall love your neighbor as yourself.' Love does no wrong to a neighbor; therefore love is the fulfilling of the law"* (Romans 13:9-10, ESV). Paul here identified the fundamental purpose and operating principle of a God-ordained government: God's model for civil government is one that **protects people from being wronged by others**. The reality is that *"not all have faith,"* as Paul wrote to the Thessalonians. There are *"wicked and evil men"* who wish to exploit, harm, and *wrong* others (2 Thessalonians 3:2, ESV). The divine model of government provides a mechanism for dealing with evil people. Personifying civil authority, Paul wrote, *"For he is God's servant for your good. But if you do wrong, be afraid, for he does not bear the sword in vain. For he is the servant of God, an avenger who carries out God's wrath on the wrongdoer"* (Romans 13:4, ESV). The job of government is to provide a peaceful atmosphere in which people may *"heartily"* do whatever they put their hands to doing (Colossians 3:23; 1 Timothy 2:2).

Those who properly understand these passages and principles understand the need to cast votes for candidates who appreciate this *limited role* that God has prescribed for civil government. Incidentally, there is a reason why the United States Constitution provides for a *limited government* with *enumerated powers:* it was composed by Bible students who understood the biblical principles expressed in this chapter.

The Christian's Vote and Moral Issues

We often have the opportunity to cast votes for candidates who are *pro-life* (anti-abortion) and *pro-marriage/pro-family* (anti-gay marriage). Some openly oppose taxpayer funded abortion and embryonic stem cell research, which Christians also oppose. Occasionally, a candidate will run on an anti-welfare platform, advocating for policies that are consistent with Paul's instructions: *"If anyone will not work, neither shall he eat"* (2 Thessalonians 3:10, NKJV). The voting booth gives us an opportunity to elect people who will make laws that are more consistent with our biblical worldview.

Considering the Character of the Candidates

Many Christians want to judge the worthiness of a candidate based upon his personal life. Marital faithfulness or infidelity are commonly cited in this regard. While it is certainly good to see a man who is faithful to his wife through the years, this does not necessarily mean that he will be a wise choice for a particular public office. Likewise, the fact that a man has been married more than once does not necessarily mean that he is unfit for a certain position.

Blamelessness in character is a Scriptural requirement for local church elders (1 Timothy 3:2; Titus 1:6-7); but appointing elders is not the same thing as voting for a candidate for a position in government. While it is understandable to want leaders who are generally moral individuals, we vote to select *civil* leaders, not *spiritual* leaders. Therefore, we ought to consider how a candidate's view on government compares with the role which God has ordained for government. It is certainly possible for one to be a faithful husband and loving father, while also seeking to use his position to usurp God's authority, ignore his divinely-ordained responsibilities, and persecute godly people.

Taxes

Godless governments often use tax money to fund immoral, ungodly, and unethical practices, as noted above. No Christian wants his tax dollars funding the abominable practice of abortion. No Christian wants to fund the farming of fetuses for medical experimentation, as is done by some embryonic stem cell researchers. We would do well to support candidates who refuse to fund such godless activities with our money.

Along with not wanting his tax dollars to fund sinful programs and practices, the Christian also knows that excessive taxation prevents him from being able to meet his God-given responsibilities towards his *family, church,* and *neighbor.* Taxation becomes punitive, confiscatory, and wrong when the tax levels reach a point where people aren't able to meet their God-given responsibilities.

The Bible tells us what is proper when it comes to paying taxes. Paul said, *"For the same reason you also pay taxes, for the authorities are ministers of God, attending to this very thing"* (Romans 13:6, RSV). What *"very thing"*? We answered this question when we earlier examined verses 3 and 4: taxes are to fund civil authorities for the purpose of *protecting those who do what is right* and for *punishing those who do what is wrong.* Notice that Paul described civil authorities as existing for our *good.* This necessarily involves the implementation of policies and laws that provide for the equal treatment of all people. The Bible teaches that it is wrong to show partiality in the treatment of others (James 2:9). Providing "equal opportunity" and a "level playing field" is no mere political sound bite: it is actually a part of God's design for civil government.

United States legislators in 2010 have wasted billions of taxpayer dollars with their so-called "stimulus act." Most of this money has been spent doing nothing close to what is authorized in Romans 13. Christians should support political candidates who understand the concept of limited taxation and who refuse to support wasteful spending.

Conclusion

Religious people make a terrible mistake when they leave the selection of public officials to atheists and humanists. Government can work effectively only when it is ordered after the divine model, and it is Bible students who understand that model. They also understand that men are known *"by their fruits"* (Matthew 7:16) and that accurate judging is done, not on the basis of *outward appearance,* but upon the basis of a *righteous standard* (John 7:24). This combination makes the Christian/Bible student the best voter.

12

KEEPING THINGS IN PERSPECTIVE

Jesus' death on the cross accomplished several things, including the atonement for sins (Ephesians 1:7) and the abolition of the Old Law (Colossians 2:14). But in His death, He also made a *"public display"* of the civil rulers and *"put them to open shame"* (Colossians 2:15). The full force of civil authority was on display against Christ. *"The kings of the earth took their stand, and the rulers were gathered together against the Lord and against His Christ"* (Acts 4:26). The result? The rulers failed. Jesus was raised from the dead, triumphing over them.

Although Jesus made a public spectacle of them, He did not abolish civil authority (Romans 13:1). We are still to be in subjection to them to a certain degree (as has already been discussed). But as we live as citizens of an earthy country, we must always keep things in perspective.

Privileges of Citizenship

Citizenship in a country usually comes with certain advantages. This is certainly true in this country. There is no reason why Christians cannot take advantage of these privileges. Paul certainly took advantage of his Roman citizenship when it was advantageous for him to do so.

- When the commander ordered that he be scourged without trial, he appealed to the fact that he was *"a Roman citizen uncondemned"* in order to escape this unjust punishment (Acts 22:24-29). Many brethren seem to have the idea that the only proper response to suffering for the cause of Christ is to silently and passively endure it. Yes, we need to be willing to suffer for the cause of Christ, just as Paul was. But when Paul could limit or avoid physical suffering, he did. In this example, he spoke up and used his citizenship as a grounds for avoiding this scourging. Elsewhere he *"fought with wild beasts"* (1 Corinthians 15:32), rather than passively allow them to tear him apart. Using the privileges afforded by citizenship to avoid suffering (rather than denying Christ to avoid suffering) does not indicate a lack of faith or an unwillingness to suffer for Christ; instead, it indicates wisdom and good sense.

- Earlier, when he was in Philippi and was wrongfully beaten and imprisoned, he used his citizenship as a way to keep the public officials accountable. When the chief magistrates begged Paul to leave the city quietly, he responded, *"They have beaten us in public without trial, men who are Romans, and have thrown us into prison; and now are they sending us away secretly? No indeed! But let them come themselves and bring us out"* (Acts 16:37). It should be noted: subjection to civil authorities does not prevent a Christian (like Paul here) from refusing to grant their request so that he could hold these authorities publicly accountable for their failures to meet God's expectations of them.

- One of the privileges that came with Roman citizenship was the ability to appeal one's case to Caesar. Paul did this (Acts 25:11-12), using the judicial system in such a way that would afford him the greatest opportunity to defend and proclaim the gospel.

We ought not be hesitant to take advantage of our citizenship today, especially as it relates to the use of our freedoms to serve God and proclaim His word. The legal and judicial systems are also there to provide certain protections when necessary. And, as was discussed in the previous chapter, we have a great privilege of being able to vote and help affect legislation and those who occupy various places in government. There is nothing improper about a Christian taking advantage of these privileges.

All Governments Will Eventually Fall

While Christians might take advantage of good conditions that exist under a particular government, we must understand that no government will last forever. The wise man wrote, "*Know well the condition of your flocks, and pay attention to your herds; for riches are not forever, nor does a crown endure to all generations*" (Proverbs 27:23-24).

No matter how stable or powerful a government may be, it will eventually fall. People in our society have come to rely upon the government for so many things, even basic necessities. It is hard for many to imagine how we could possibly survive without our government in its current form. Yet the wise man tells us how we can survive: work hard, be good stewards, and trust in God and in His providence (Proverbs 27:23-27). Governments rise and fall, as they have done since their beginning and will continue to do until the end of time. God's provisions will remain.

It is important to remember that no human government is exempt from this rule. When Daniel interpreted Nebuchadnezzar's dream about the statue made up of gold, silver, bronze, iron, and clay, he prophesied of four world empires: the Babylonians, the Medes and the Persians, the Greeks, and the Romans (Daniel 2:31-43). Each one of these mighty nations fell. Even our current government, despite its great success over the last two hundred twenty-five years, will not be around forever.

Christ's Kingdom Will Endure Forever

In contrast with these four human kingdoms, Daniel tells of another kingdom — one that would come from God.

> *"In the days of those kings the God of heaven will set up a kingdom which will never be destroyed, and that kingdom will not be left for another people; it will crush and put an end to all these kingdoms, but it will itself endure forever"* (Daniel 2:44).

Unlike the other kingdoms, this one would be established by God, and its King would be Christ (John 18:36-37). Jesus told His disciples, *"The gates of Hades will not overpower"* His kingdom (Matthew 16:18). It would endure until *"the end, when [Christ] hands over the kingdom to the God and Father, when He has abolished all rule and all authority and power"* (1 Corinthians 15:24).

Our Citizenship Is In Heaven

We certainly enjoy numerous blessings of citizenship in this country. We ought to be mindful of these things, thankful for them, and, as Paul did with his Roman citizenship, speak out in defense of them and take advantage of them.

But first and foremost, our primary citizenship is in heaven. Paul wrote, *"For our citizenship is in heaven, from which also we eagerly wait for a Savior, the Lord Jesus Christ; who will transform the body of our humble state into conformity with the body of His glory, by the exertion of the power that He has even to subject all things to Himself"* (Philippians 3:20-21).

Paul says we *eagerly* look forward to Christ's return. We have a great reward waiting for us in heaven (1 Peter 1:4). No matter what we have here or how many privileges come with our earthly citizenship, it cannot compare with what we will receive in heaven (Matthew 16:26).

APPENDIX

THE BIBLE AGAINST SOCIALISM AND COMMUNISM

Karl Marx defined socialism as the step between *capitalism* and *communism*. Under socialism, all property and means of production are owned and controlled by the society (the community). Of course, without free-market forces balancing supply and demand, some person or group of people must eventually plan the economy. This opens the door to the *central planning* of communistic or other totalitarian forms of government. For central planning to work, all members of the collective must allow the planners to make all decisions about what is to be produced, grown, and manufactured. Planners must also be allowed to decide *how much* of each item is produced. In the past, miscalculations, ineptitude, inefficiency, and indifference on the part of the planners has resulted in the starvation deaths of millions of people. It should also be noted that socialism empowers the ruling class to direct state-sponsored violence and persecution against potential threats to the system. History contains many examples of such persecution being directed against people on the basis of political, ethnic, and religious differences. Along with the millions who have starved to death because of socialistic policies, millions of others have been deliberately slaughtered.

Regardless of this history, there are those in every generation who idealistically believe in the concept of socialism. Their utopian dream hinders them from accepting the logical development of socialism into communism. Marx, Engels, and others understood the inevitability of this transition quite well, and history contains many tragic examples of its effects. Since the writings of Marx and Engels, many nations have experimented with various forms of socialism and everywhere it has been tried it has failed. Oddly, however, even with this history there are still plenty of people and nations who are willing to try it again. Blind personal pride leads some people to believe that socialism will work if only *they* are the ones doing it. They reason that socialism has failed in the past only because the wrong people have tried it. Such idealists ignore the fact that the very concept of socialism is inherently flawed and contrary to God's economic model. God ordained the function of government (Romans 13:3-4; 1 Timothy 2:2; 1 Peter 2:14). He did not ordain food production or economic control as a part of that function.

Why Use The Bible To Refute Socialism?

Some might wonder why I would approach this subject from a biblical perspective. Socialism is usually refuted on a purely secular and logical basis. The only "moral" component to such secular arguments is that a *man is entitled to the fruits of his labor*. It is my belief that this moral argument is actually best made by the Bible, and that regardless of one's view of Bible inspiration, its simple observations on this subject are compelling and its logic is irrefutable. Because of its emphasis on personal responsibility, the Bible has much to say about work and economy. Even those who reject the *verbal inspiration* of the Scriptures can still appreciate its pragmatic treatment of basic human responsibilities and interaction.

Another reason to use the Bible in this refutation is to answer those who *misuse* the Bible in their effort to defend socialism and communism. Given the connection between *atheism* and *socialism*, and the disdain that Marxists generally have for religion, I am surprised to see how much effort they exert in trying to prove that the Bible supports socialism. Certain verses from Acts chapters 2 and 4 are regularly cited by socialists, though as we shall see, they disregard the context of those chapters and ignore the peculiar circumstances. Barack Obama recently cited part of Luke 12:48 in an effort to defend the practice of income redistribution. Jesus said in this verse, "...*for everyone to whom much is given, from him much will be required...*" (NKJV). Though it has absolutely nothing at all to do with *government* action of collecting and reallocating personal income, President Obama and others cite the passage in an effort to defend redistributionist policies. Another man recently cited Matthew 5:40 as proof that Jesus favored a 100% income tax. Jesus said, "*If any man wants to sue you and take your shirt, let him have your coat also.*" The socialist's poor interpretive skills are rivaled only by his lack of mathematical skills. For his application of the passage to be correct, he needs the government to be the plaintiff (though Jesus said he was "*a man*"), and needs the defendant to possess only his shirt and coat and nothing else. (Did the man not have sandals or even a sash?) Socialists obviously don't make good Bible scholars. Of course, they aren't sincere in their approach to the Bible. A genuine socialist will say and do whatever is necessary to protect and advance the collective. To him there is no "right" or "wrong" — there is merely the progress of the state.

Inherent Flaws Of Socialism

Socialism Results In Loss Of Personal Liberty: In the absence of supply-and-demand, the economy must be controlled by some person or group of people. In order to control the economy this person or group must control the laborers (the people). Thus, the loss of a free-market economy is linked inexorably to the loss of personal liberty. There are logical reasons why communist states do not permit freedom of expression or freedom of movement. Tyrants know that when freedoms are allowed in small areas (thought, artistic expression, speech, and movement), then people will desire freedom in larger, more important areas (religious expression, family size, type of occupation, work schedule, place and type of residence, etc). In a planned economy/society these decisions are made by the planners of the ruling class. A controlled economy can function properly only if people are *where they are told to be, doing what they are told to do.* Any deviation from this arrangement has the potential to disrupt the health and harmony of the society, even to the point of jeopardizing its very existence. Members of the collective must cede their liberties to the collective in order for the system to function properly.

James 4:13 illustrates the total *freedom* of the divine model of economy. The man of this scenario chooses the *place* where he wishes to do business (goes into *"such and such a city"*). He decides *how long* he will stay there (*"spend a year there"*). He chooses the *type of work* that he will do (*"buy and sell,"* NKJV), and he *makes a profit* as a result of his own *personal business decisions.* Socialism does not allow for such choices by the individual, and it literally *despises* the "profit" making that is discussed in this passage. Even the less extreme *democratic socialism* that the United States is now toying with is antagonistic to *profit-making.* To the socialist, all "profit-making" is "obscene" and "immoral."

While at Philippi, Paul met certain women at the riverside where they assembled for prayer. Among these women was a woman from Thyatira named Lydia. She, along with her family, was visiting Philippi. Luke describes her as *"a seller of purple fabrics"* (Acts 16:14). Lydia was a business-woman who had obviously travelled from Thyatira to Philippi in search of another or better market for her product. Freedom *of movement* allowed Lydia to expand her business. Socialism restricts movement, and is thus contrary to these Bible examples. Along with *religious freedom*, Lydia enjoyed *economic freedom.* These freedoms provide the ideal environment for humans to lead the *"tranquil and quiet"* lives that God would have them to live (1 Timothy 2:2).

In His parable of the great pearl, Jesus described a merchant, who *"upon finding one pearl of great value, he went and sold all that he had and bought it"* (Matthew 13:45-46). This is an example of *free-market capitalism*. The merchant made his own economic decision based upon his own comparative evaluation of the items involved. He estimated the value of the *great pearl* to be high enough to justify his selling everything else that he owned in order to buy it. Socialism does not allow individuals such power of economic choice. As we shall see, socialism violates personal free-agency. In the above examples, each person made his own decision about where and how he would conduct his business. Socialist-styled *planned economies* do not grant people such liberties.

The pie-in-the-sky utopian may love the notion of being supported by the collective, but he fails to consider the cost to him in the loss of personal liberties. Many socialist-leaning youths enjoy their smart phones, tablets, X-Boxes, Play Stations and televisions. I wonder if they have stopped to consider just how such devices might be viewed by authoritarian leaders? Is it possible that totalitarian central-planners might view such devices as a *waste of time* and *threat to society?* Might they consider that the time that youths spend playing computer games might be better spent in work and production? History answers my questions with a resounding yes — that is precisely what they would think. Even books were banished under Hitler's national socialism, under the fear that certain writings might inspire free thought. Collectivist economic models may sound good, but only in theory. In reality they rob people of their personal liberties.

Socialism Is Contrary To Free Agency: Socialism is antithetical to the very nature of both God and man. By creating man in His own image (Genesis 1:26-27), God created man with perfect *free-agency* — the power to choose. Religious people often speak of free "moral" agency, but "moral" choices aren't the only choices that free agency allows. We also make many other choices — from the mate that we choose and the jobs that we do, to the type of clothing that we wear and vehicles that we drive. Native free-agency is not just "a religious thing." It is that quality of human nature that identifies him and allows him to distinguish himself from all others. It causes him to crave and appreciate freedom in all facets of life. It is individuality. Free agency is one of our greatest gifts from God. Socialists hate the notion of "rugged individualism," for it emphasizes the strength of the individual over the collective. Under socialism and communism, personal freedom is sacrificed for the "greater good" of government and society. Human free-agency is over- ruled by the needs of the collective. In the words of the "Spock" character in one of the Star Trek movies, in collectivism, "the needs of the many outweigh the needs of the few."

Socialism Is Dispiriting: The divine model of economy is designed upon man's innate free agency. Each man is personally responsible for his own livelihood and that of his family. This need for him to provide for himself and his family provides a strong personal incentive for him to work and succeed. If one wishes to eat, then he must work (2 Thessalonians 3:10). Adam was told that he would produce food from the ground through painful exertion — *"in toil you will eat of it... by the sweat of your face you will eat bread..."* (Genesis 3:17, 19). The slothful man acquires nothing (Proverbs 13:4). The diligent man is rewarded (Proverbs 12:24; Ephesians 4:28). *Socialism is contrary to God's design, for under socialism the slothful man is rewarded like the diligent man.* Each one receives his livelihood from the collective. There is no advantage or benefit to working harder than anyone else, for the reward is the same either way. I remember several years ago, going with my brothers to look at a Russian-made Belarus tractor. I commented to them that the axle housing and other parts were very roughly finished. My middle brother responded, *"What do you expect: It was built by a bunch of drunk Russians!"* Some time after that, I read a news report about the utter hopelessness of Russian workers and how large numbers of them drowned their despair in vodka every night. Government programs had to be formed to discourage so much alcohol consumption! Socialism breeds apathy and despair; and ironically, these are conditions that socialism cannot itself repair.

The redistributionist policies of *democratic socialism* are just as spirit-crushing as those of full-blown socialism. The entrepreneurial spirit is extinguished through excessive regulation and taxation. Under redistributionism, money must be increasingly confiscated from producers in order to satisfy the needs and wants of the non-producers. Oftentimes politically fueled, this policy leads to class warfare, essentially dividing the population into the classes of *makers* and *takers*. The makers begin to resent that the fruits of their long hours and extra effort are forcibly taken and given to those who put forth little or no effort. The takers resent the fact that the makers possess the things that they do. It is a recipe for social disaster.

If the simple biblical principles of taxation were followed, this class divide would be greatly reduced. Sure, there will always be people who are jealous, envious, and covetous; but there would be no *government* framework for encouraging and accommodating their sinful attitudes. Under the biblical model of taxation, taxes are paid in order to provide civil authorities with the ability to *punish those who do evil* and to *protect those who do good* (Romans 13:3-7; 1 Peter 2:14). Under the divine model, taxpayers pay for whatever services fit within this divinely authorized framework. A criminal justice system, a standing military force, various levels and types of law enforcement and fire and emergency services are just a few things that come to my mind when considering these categories. The basic God-ordained functions of government are a service to every citizen, thus every citizen should pay some amount of tax (Romans 13:6-7). Class warfare would be greatly minimized if all citizens paid at least some tax, for all would have a personal interest in how their money was being used.

Socialism Ignores Differences In Work Ethic: Different people have different work ethics. Experience and observation tell us that some people work *harder* than other people. Some people work *smarter* than other people, and some people work *longer* than other people. Paul and his companions labored and toiled "*night and day*" that they might not be burdensome to anyone (1 Thessalonians 2:9). Contrariwise, the Bible describes some as being "*slothful*" and "*sluggards.*" The sluggard is one who *sleeps too much* (Proverbs 6:9). "*As the door turns upon its hinges, so does the sluggard on his bed*" (Proverbs 26:14). He refuses to work (Proverbs 21:25), especially under any conditions that he deems to be too harsh (Proverbs 20:4 — "*does not plow after the autumn*"). He makes any possible excuse for not meeting his responsibilities, even exaggerating and imagining potential obstacles — "*there is a lion outside; I will be killed in the streets!*" (Proverbs 22:13; 26:13). He is undependable and unreliable (Proverbs 10:26). He is so lazy that he will not even roast his game after it is caught (Proverbs 12:27). Consequently, he "*gets nothing*" (Proverbs 13:4). First century Cretans had the reputation of being "*lazy gluttons*" (Titus 1:12).

In His parable of the talents, Jesus describes an investor dispersing various weights (amounts) of money to three different men according to their ability. One man was given five talents, another was given two, and another was given one. The five and two talent men each doubled their master's investment, but the one talent man hid his money and made no increase. Upon his return, the investor commended the five and two talent men, but he condemned the one talent man for his *slothfulness*. The one talent man was to be cast out into outer darkness where he would experience "*weeping and gnashing of teeth*" (Matthew 25:14-30). Under socialistic models of economy, the one talent man would have been given equal share with the five and two talent men.

This is not so under Christ's model. Under His model of economy, each person profits according to his own level of work and commitment.

Socialism Rewards Irresponsibility: The more that people and societies drift away from the mores of a biblical and traditional worldview, the less personally responsible they are and the more dependent upon others they become. Rather than working *"with* [their] *hands"* (1 Thessalonians 4:11), eating *"their own bread"* (2 Thessalonians 3:12) and being *"dependent on no one"* (1 Thessalonians 4:12, ESV), such people look to others for their sustenance. Far too many able-bodied and sound-minded people turn to family members (usually parents), churches, charitable organizations, or government agencies for their livelihood. This has a debilitating effect upon societies, leading to their eventual demise. The apostle Paul told the Thessalonians that any man who refuses to work should not eat (2 Thessalonians 3:10).[1]

The notion of "sharing" certainly sounds good, and the Bible teaches us to share with those who have need. But the forced "sharing" of collectivism is not taught in the Bible. In contrasting love that is *"in word and talk"* with love that is *"in deed and truth,"* John wrote, *"But if anyone has the world's goods and sees his brother in need, but closes his heart against him, how does God's love abide in him?"* (1 John 3:17-18, ESV). Clearly, a part of loving one's brother or neighbor is helping him physically when he needs such help. This is well demonstrated in the parable of the good Samaritan (Luke 10:30-37). However, the "sharing" of

---

[1] Please note that I am discussing the duties of capable individuals, not of those who are incapable. People can become debilitated, either physically or mentally, and therefore be unable to support themselves. They can also be the victims of a bad economy or of detrimental government policies, such as over-regulation and excessive taxation, which stifle free enterprise and destroy opportunity. It is right and good for the capable to help the disabled, the sick and the infirm. The focus of this article is upon those who do have ability and opportunity but seek to evade that responsibility.

collectivism is not the kind-hearted caring and sharing of the good Samaritan. Even if started with the best of intentions, collectivism rapidly degenerates into totalitarianism, for someone (usually a charismatic leader or particular political party) will soon emerge to make decisions for the collective. This usually ends with the deaths of thousands to millions of innocent people.

Paul's Three Classifications
Ephesians 4:28

The apostle Paul told the Ephesians, *"Let the thief no longer steal, but rather let him labor, doing honest work with his own hands, so that he may have something to share with anyone in need"* (ESV).

Paul identifies three classifications of people with respect to supply of needs:

1. The *thief* who wrongly satisfies his need by taking from others.
2. The *laborer* who rightly satisfies his need through his own honest labor.
3. The *legitimately needy person* whose condition authorizes him to take from others. (*Note: One might become "needy" as a result of his own laziness and foolishness. Paul told the Thessalonians that if one is unwilling to work, then neither should he eat — 2 Thessalonians 3:10. Unlike the slacker of this passage, the needy person of Ephesians 4:28 was obviously worthy to receive assistance from others.*)

1. Types of Thievery

When one thinks of a "thief" he usually thinks of one who breaks into someone's house or place of business and steals items that he can either use for himself or sell for cash. The thief may be the sneaky, non-violent "cat" burglar type, who poses no personal physical threat to property owners. The Bible says, *"Men do not despise a thief if he steals to satisfy himself when he is hungry"* (Proverbs 6:30). This passage does not condone theft, but it does show that some thieves are different than others. It depicts an extenuating circumstance that might be taken into consideration when rendering legal judgment or administering punishment. This type of thief is certainly different from the dangerous, armed invader who has no respect for human life and will harm or kill his victims in an act of theft. While the word "thief" may suggest these ordinary types of thieves, there are other kinds of thievery that we should be concerned about.

The 8th Mosaic Commandment was, *"You shall not steal"* (Exodus 20:15; Romans 13:9). This commandment presupposes the right of **personal property ownership.** *(There could be no "theft" if not for the right of personal property possession.)* This same observation can be made about Paul's words in Ephesians 4:28. One is to work with his hands what is good so that he may *"have something"* to share with anyone in need. Notice that the worker *has something.* The fruits of his labor are his own possession to either use for himself or give to others.

Theft is wrong because one's possessions, whether acquired by gift or by labor, are his own property. The thief believes that he is somehow entitled to the possessions, wealth and income of others, so he takes it. Under collectivist systems like socialism and communism, the God-given right of personal property ownership is rejected. All means of production and all produce are owned and controlled by the collective (community leaders or central government). The state (or collective) confiscates all personal wealth, and it redistributes the wealth as it sees fit. *Socialistic and communistic systems of economy are based upon theft.* As such, they are anti-God and contrary to the divinely revealed model of economy. The idealist may argue that this is not necessarily the case and that a socialistic economy could be formed upon mutual agreement by the members of the society. However, as explained before, both history and logic prove such to be impossible, at least for a sustained period of time, for the "mutual sharing" of the dreamer's collective soon transitions to the planned economy of rank and ruthless socialism.

Some people deny being socialists, yet they support the practice of *income redistribution*. During the 2008 Presidential campaign, Barack Obama notoriously told Joe the Plumber that it is good "to spread the wealth around." In context, he meant that he thought it was good to take money from one group of people and give it to another. However, like socialism, the doctrine and practice of income redistribution is based upon *theft*. Some entity (usually government) confiscates wealth from one group of people and distributes it to another group. Their goal is to achieve parity. This process is known in modern terms as "social justice."[2]

2. The Value of Labor

As seen from the above passages, it is God's will for men to work to provide for themselves and for others: *"But if anyone does not provide for his relatives, and especially for members of his household, he has denied the faith and is worse than an unbeliever"* (1 Timothy 5:8, ESV).

This is an interesting statement in view of the spiritual consequences of unbelief: Mark 16:16 and 2 Thessalonians 2:12

---

[2] An observation about labels: The apparent sinfulness of a thing is often concealed by calling it by another name. While it may be "social," there is nothing "just" about tyrants or governments stealing money from one person in order to give it to another person. As the commentator/economist Walter E. Williams so well explains, one will be charged with theft if he forcibly takes money from a person, even if his intent is to give the stolen money to another less fortunate person. Yet governments do this all of the time! They take money from one person and give it to another person. I should point out that, like Barack Obama, Walter Williams is a black man. Their color makes no difference to me, but it might make a difference to others who might assume me to be "racist" for criticizing President Obama's social ideology.

both say that people will be *"damned"* for unbelief. Paul's point is obvious: the refusal to support one's family is as wrong as unbelief. Even infidels support their families. One cannot retain his character as a Christian while refusing to support his family.

We earlier saw from Ephesians 4:28 that one is to work so that he can provide for his own needs and for the needs of others. Paul was himself an example in this regard:

> *"You yourselves know that these hands ministered to my own needs and to the men who were with me"* (Acts 20:34)

> *"For you recall, brethren, our labor and hardship, how working night and day so as not to be a burden to any of you..."* (1 Thessalonians 2:9).

What an amazing contrast to so many millions of people in North America, France, Greece and elsewhere! I recently heard that the United States now has over 100 million people on some type of government welfare. Notice that not only did Paul and his companions *work* — but they worked *hard, long hours*. We are reminded of the parable of the vineyard laborers in Matthew 20:1-16. We know that the workday consisted of 12 hours, for those hired in the eleventh hour worked one hour (11 + 1 = 12). We also know that the Jewish work-week consisted of 6 days (Exodus 20:9). Thus they worked six 12-hour days. Many people in this country complain if they have to work any more than 40 hours per week. This begs the question: *Who invented the concept of a 40-hour work-week?* It certainly is not a *biblical* concept! Sadly, North American youths have been literally brainwashed into this concept. Some simply refuse to work any more than forty hours per week. Listening to some of them, you would think that they had received some type of divine exemption from working more than the magical *forty hours* per week! Some European countries have standard work-weeks of 35 hours or less. Not surprisingly, these very countries are now bankrupt and are facing terrible social unrest from their spoiled work forces. Such people complain and protest, yet their work-week is one half of the standard Jewish work-week under the Mosaic economy. Those who complain about "how rich those Jews are" might want to consider their work ethic before making judgmental statements against them.

The "privileged" mentality and cultural laziness is not a new development. The apostle Paul quoted a Cretan prophet as saying, "*Cretans are always liars, evil beasts and lazy gluttons.*" Paul confirmed the accuracy of the prophet's statement, saying, "*This testimony is true. For this reason reprove them severely so that they may be sound in the faith*" (Titus 1:12-13). The condition in first century Crete demonstrates how a lack of personal responsibility can become culturally engrained. The dependency mentality becomes generational. Each new generation learns laziness and irresponsibility from the previous generation. The condition is self-perpetuating so long as there is government or others who are willing to subsidize this lifestyle. Sadly, ethnicity and race considerations make it taboo to criticize the welfare culture. This makes the condition virtually impossible to change.

The Fruits of One's Labor

Adam was to produce his food in *pain* and *sweat* (Genesis 3:17-19). Paul and the vineyard workers worked long, hard hours. There was, however, the sweet satisfaction that the fruits of their labor were their own to use, share, and enjoy. Though he did warn against the vain toil of mere material acquisition, Solomon did teach that one should take *joy* and *pleasure* in his toil (Ecclesiastes 2:24; 3:13, 22). That is, he should "*eat and drink and enjoy the good of all his labor*" (Ecclesiastes 3:13, NKJV). Solomon said these fruits were *man's lot* and *God's gift to man*. **Socialism robs man of this God-given gift** — it takes the fruits of one man's labor and disperses them to other men. As stated before, this constitutes theft.

As seen from the examples of Adam, Paul, and others, the food that they produced and the money that they earned was their own to use as they saw fit. This is well demonstrated in the case of Ananias and Sapphira (Acts 5:1-11). This married couple sold a piece of property and gave part of the proceeds to the church (Acts 5:1-2). Tragically, they represented themselves as having given *all* of the proceeds when in fact they had given only part. They committed no sin by giving only part of the proceeds, nor did they sin by owning or selling property. Their sin was that of *lying*. They lied about the amount (percentage) of money that they had given to the church. Peter told Ananias, "*While it remained unsold, did it not remain your own? And after it was sold, was it not under your control? Why is it that you have conceived this deed in your heart? You have not lied to men but to God*" (Acts 5:4).

Of course, the primary purpose of this story is to show that God condemns lying and misrepresentation. However, the lesson is also taught that God grants humans the right to own and control property. Under collectivism, all property, means of production, produce, and income are owned by the collective. The individual *cedes control of his life, liberty, and property to the leaders of the collective* (usually some tyrant or tyrannical political party or board); and they assume responsibility over the people. Neither socialism nor communism fit the divine model of personal rights and responsibility. Socialism actually breeds irresponsibility. It never encourages personal initiative, ambition or productivity.

3. Helping The Needy

Under collectivist models of economy, the directors of the collective decide how the money is spent. Karl Marx's slogan was, "*From each according to his ability, to each according to his need.*"

This always sounds great in theory; but in order for it to be implemented some person or group of people must define the classes ("able" versus "needy") and decide the parameters of (re) distribution. Currently in the United States, a family of four is considered impoverished if it has an annual income of $23,000.00 or less. Millions of "impoverished" people in the United States have adequate housing, never go hungry, own at least one automobile and at least one flat screen television, and have cable or satellite television. Obviously, the expression "poverty level" is a relative term. "Impoverished" people of other countries don't do quite so well.

Under the policies of democratic socialism (which the United States is rapidly advancing toward), those under the "poverty level" are subsidized by the fruits of other people's labor. The collective takes from one class and gives to another. This is accomplished through a graduated tax code, which in the United States has resulted in the top 50% of federal taxpayers paying 98% of the taxes. The top 10% pays 70% of all federal taxes, and the top 1% pays a whopping 37% of all federal taxes! Through burdensome taxation, the government redistributes money from the wealthier class to the poorer class through a variety of government assistance and welfare programs. The term "government assistance" is far more accurate than one might initially think, for a large part of the "assistance" goes to "government" workers. Multiple layers of bureaucracy siphon off billions of the tax dollars that are taken from the producers and given to non-producers.

Under the biblical model of economy, the *individual* decides how much money he will give and to whom he will give it. This brings us full circle back to the principle of free agency. Our giving is an expression of our personal free agency. Ephesians 4:28 says that the laborer *"will have something to share with one who has need."* Jesus tells us to *"give to him who asks"* (Matthew 5:42). The good Samaritan personally aided the attack victim, even telling the innkeeper, *"Take care of him; and whatever more you spend, when I return I will repay you"* (Luke 10:35). In worship giving, *"Each one...is to put aside ans save, as he may prosper..."* (1 Corinthians 16:2). *"Each one must do just as he has purposed in his heart, not grudgingly or under compulsion, for God loves a cheerful giver"* (2 Corinthians 9:7). As we have opportunity we are to *"do good to all people, and especially to those who are of the household of faith"* (Galatians 6:10). The "giving" of collectivism violates the free-will principle of giving that is taught in Scripture.

The Sharing Of Acts 2 & 4

Some people claim that the Bible promotes and encourages socialism and even communism. They cite the "sharing" passages of Acts chapters 2 and 4 as evidence of a *communistic* lifestyle. The argument is made primarily from Acts 2:44-45 and Acts 4:32:

> *"And all who believed were together and had all things in common. And they were selling their possessions and belongings and distributing the proceeds to all, as any had need"* (Acts 2:44-45, ESV).

> *"Now the full number of those who believed were of one heart and one soul, and no one said that any of the things that belonged to him were his own, but they had everything in common"* (Acts 4:32, ESV).

It is alleged from these statements that first century Christians practiced what is called *community of property* — a system in which all property, production, and proceeds are ceded to a common pool and distribution is made to each person according to his need. Some have compared these conditions in the early church to the communistic doctrine that was popularized by Karl Marx's slogan, *"From each according to his ability, to each according to his need."* However, *Marxism* is not what was practiced by first century Christians. Such an interpretation of Acts 2 and 4 disparages the kindness and generosity of first century saints, reducing their sacrifice to a mere communal obligation. A Bible story that is intended as an example of good and virtuous acts of free-will giving and love for neighbor is hijacked by liberals who will do anything they can to establish a system of income redistribution. They will happily distort biblical narrative if it means advancing their socialist agenda. Honest Bible students respect *context*, whereas those who are interested only in advancing some ideology will misuse sacred texts in order to advance their godless agendas.

Some Important Observations

First, Acts 2 describes a once-in-history occurrence — the establishment of the Lord's church. This will never happen again. Jewish males had convened in Jerusalem to observe Pentecost, but they found themselves being exposed to the first gospel sermon. Thousands of them obeyed the gospel and continued in Jerusalem (Acts 2:37ff.). Their extended stay in Jerusalem placed an unusual financial burden upon the Jews who resided in that area. Native Jews sold even their *lands and houses* in order to assist their new brothers (Acts 4:34). The conditions of Acts 2-5 will never again be duplicated, so great care must be taken when interpreting these passages.

Second, the proceeds were *"laid...at the apostles' feet"* (Acts 4:35; 5:2, ESV). This expression implies a treasury, but not that of a human board or central-planning committee. The money was contributed to the Lord's *church* (Acts 5:11), not to the government. Funds were distributed under the oversight of the *church*, not of an economic planning board.

People sold their property in order to assist their *needy* brethren (Acts 2:44,45; 4:32-5:1). The Bible defines a "needy" person as one who lacks food and clothing. Paul said, *"And having food and clothing, with these we shall be content"* (1 Timothy 6:8, NKJV). By helping the "needy," the giver provided food and clothing. The parable of the good Samaritan expands this to include *shelter* and *medical care* (Luke 10:30-35). This aid was provided by the free-will offerings of individual Christians. The decisions were not made by the community or by some government panel or political party. The second and fourth chapters of Acts teach us lessons about *brotherly love* and *generosity*, not about socialism or communism!

Conclusion

While the concept of "community sharing" sounds like a great idea, socialism and communism are not merely about sharing — they are about *control*. Humans tend to want to control and regulate other humans. This ranges from the simple "control freak" who is intent upon running other people's lives, to the megalomaniac who seeks to control the world. Socialism seeks to control and regulate the fruits of man's labor. By controlling the fruits of one's labor, one controls the laborer. According to the Bible, God grants each human the possession and control of the fruits of his own labor. As free agents, we can use this wealth in a way that redounds to the glory of God (Matthew 19:21; 2 Corinthians 9:13); or we can use it for our own godless self-pleasure (Luke 12:16-21; 15:13; 16:19-24). Though God allows us to make the choice, He holds us accountable for the decisions we make (2 Corinthians 5:10).

Obviously, socialism would not be so appealing if all one knew of it was that it enabled some people to obtain total control over others. There is another, more deceptive dimension to it: socialism appeals to man's desire to be cared for and provided for by someone else. It frightens man to think that he is responsible for his own life and livelihood. Socialism offers him security (though at great costs in personal liberty). The state promises to feed him when he is hungry, clothe and shelter him when he is cold, and cure him when he is sick. The term "nanny state" has been appropriately applied to this arrangement. As the child takes comfort in the arms of his mother, so the citizen (better, *denizen*) takes comfort in the arms of the state. Herein lies the great and dangerous deception — unlike a child's mother, the monolithic mechanism of the state lacks the capacity to provide personal care for its "child." The collective's real purpose is not to defend and preserve the rights of individuals, but to strengthen and promote itself. Christians must oppose socialism and communism, for these systems of economy and governance are contrary to God's design of both man, government, and economy.

www.ingramcontent.com/pod-product-compliance
Lightning Source LLC
Chambersburg PA
CBHW051824040426
42447CB00006B/360